GARDEN WISDOM

GARDEN WISDOM

Compiled by Leslie Geddes-Brown

Illustrations by Angie Lewin

MERRELL

LONDON · NEW YORK

Introduction

Any gardener who thinks he knows it all cannot be a good gardener. No gardener will ever know it all. All of us who garden understand that what seemed once to be an unbreakable rule may be suddenly overturned by scientists or, more likely, by Nature herself. This may be where the traditional Mr McGregors get it wrong: they have their rules, which have been passed down to them by the head gardeners under whom they trained, and, in their turn, they will pass their knowledge on to their own staff. Good, as far as it goes, but in nature, rules have a habit of changing.

I remember talking to a gardener who had started life designing shoes and was scornfully critical of all this professional received wisdom. He worked near Truro in Cornwall, where the council had planted groups of palms, both hardy and tender. Cornwall, on England's south-west tip, has the best climate in these islands, and tender plants were thought to be safe. Of course, this being Britain, there was eventually a long, hard frost. The professional gardeners got a nasty surprise: the hardy palms all succumbed, and those thought to be tender survived. The professionals' wisdom was overturned.

This is where garden writers come in. In the hazy days of the head gardener and his team, there were few garden writers, and most of them were in the inflexible Mr McGregor mould. They weren't interested in design or aesthetics but in 'the answer lies in the soil' approach. Any amateur reading their books would never, from either terror or boredom, put hand to spade. Perhaps that was the idea. Alternatively, gardens were designed by architects, who were equally dismissive of the amateur.

With the arrival of Gertrude Jekyll at the beginning of the twentieth century, the rules changed. Jekyll was inspired by English cottage gardens, in much the same way as her collaborator, Sir Edwin Lutyens, was by vernacular architecture. Jekyll was an artist, and saw plants as part of an overall design, while Lutyens added the structural bones to hold her planting together. She wrote articles and books for *Country Life*, complete with detailed planting plans that could be copied by the lady of the manor (Jekyll's book on small country-house gardens required two acres).

A hundred years on, there are books for every kind of temperate garden, and in picking these excerpts, I have learned a great deal. Though some are chosen for beginners – and we were all beginners once – there's plenty here to give even experienced gardeners a hint or two, or a nasty shock when they find they have been doing it all wrong, just like the men in Truro.

Many of the extracts were written in the last fifty years, largely because gardening, like architecture or cooking, is influenced by fashion. Who now copies the Victorian bedding schemes except Waddesdon Manor's National Trust gardens in Buckinghamshire, where there is Rothschild money to apply this most artificial of designs? Who plans slate rockeries in the style of the 1930s, bringing the Welsh mountains to suburban Stockbroker Tudor homes? Who has the island beds so beloved of the 1960s? Or the dwarf conifers? Or those municipal beds commemorating some civic pride or other? All as dated as the knot garden and the succession house.

But I have included the giants of the recent past whose views still inspire us: those who changed our direction, from William Robinson, with his flowery meadow planting, to Margery Fish, who valued small and delicate cottage plants. Of course, there's Vita Sackville-West, perhaps the principal figure of the twentieth century (though her husband, Harold Nicolson, did as much as she). Vita's name is better known because she wrote about her efforts in a column in *The Observer* newspaper, as did that supreme iconoclast Christopher Lloyd, who thought nothing of uprooting his parents' sacred rose-garden and planting it with tropical cannas. He wrote weekly in *Country Life* for decades.

I have chosen each extract to be practical. No violins at sunset here, but at least one pure 24-carat nugget per extract, whether it be on plants, planting or design – and generally, I hope, a positive mother lode of advice from practising gardeners.

I worried that when I started to search for extracts I would find I ran out of subjects; that pages would be given to, for example, old-fashioned roses, about which everyone has an opinion. This was not the case at all: there is so much to say about gardens. The severely practical, such as composting, watering and weeding; the propagating from cuttings, layers or seeds; the joys of plants, such as their textures, their pasts, their scents and flowers; the passions a single type of plant – such as ferns, tulips and magnolias – can arouse. There are excerpts on design and its tricks, such as false perspective, and how to use water. There was never any chance that I would run out of subjects.

The whole book was, in its turn, inspired by the art of Angie Lewin, who brings her own vision of the natural world to her work. She sees the beauty in all seasons and all manifestations of plants: the ordered pattern of the blooms, the thrusting energy of the emerging buds, the prolific seed heads and the varieties of shapes, colours and habits to be found in meadow and border.

Angie's chosen plants tend to the wild, less well-bred kinds, such as honesty seed heads and teasels, once used for teasing cloth. She favours goat's beard and dandelions, alexanders, cow parsley and garlic flowers. These are the plants of the herbalist, the monastery garden, and of the wild cliff tops of Britain: plants that cure illnesses, flavour casseroles, and fill earthenware jugs in country cottages.

To look at Angie's prints is an inspiration in itself. You are made aware of the complexity and beauty of nature and, with the addition of these extracted words of wisdom from dozens of gardeners, you will grow your own plants with new enthusiasm. Perhaps, after all, the answer does lie in the soil.

LESLIE GEDDES-BROWN

THE PLACE

Lettuce delighteth to grow, as Palladius saith, in a mannured, fat, moist and dunged ground: it must be sowen in faire weather in places where there is plenty of water, as Columella saith, and prospereth best if it be sowen very thin.

THE TIME

It is certaine, saith Palladius, that Lettuce may well be sowen at any time of the yeare, but especially at every first Spring, and so soone as Winter is done, till Summer be well nigh spent.

THE NAMES

Garden Lettuce is called in Latine, *Lactuca sativa*, of the milky juice which issueth forth of the wounded stalkes and roots.

THE TEMPERATURE

Lettuce is a cold and moist pot-herbe, yet not in the extream degree of cold or moisture, but altogether moderately; for otherwise it were not to be eaten.

THE VERTUES

Lettuce cooleth the heat of the stomacke, called the heart-burning; and helpeth it when it is troubled with choler: it quencheth thirst and causeth sleepe.

Lettuce maketh a pleasant sallad, being eaten raw with vinegar, oile, and a little salt: but if it be boiled it is sooner digested, and nourisheth more.

It is served in these daies, and in these countries in the beginning of supper, and eaten first before any other meat: which also Martiall testifieth to be done in his time, marvelling why some did use it for a service at the end of supper, in these verses.

'Tell me why Lettuce, which our Grandsires last did eat,

Is now of late become, to be the first of meat?'

Notwithstanding it may now and then be eaten at both those times to the health of the body: for being taken before meat it doth many times stir up appetite: and eaten after supper it keepeth away drunkenesse which commeth by the wine; and that is by reason that it staieth the vapours from rising up into the head.

John Gerard
The Complete Herball
1633

The Right Gardener

The moral of this excerpt by WILLIAM GEORGE SPENCER CAVENDISH
(1790–1858), 6TH DUKE OF DEVONSHIRE, *is to find the right gardener.*
He found Joseph Paxton, young and untried, hired him as chief gardener at Chatsworth
in Derbyshire, and, as he describes in this extract, saw the grounds change out of
all recognition. The two men became firm friends. Paxton was later knighted
for creating the Crystal Palace in London.

Joseph Paxton was born the 3rd August 1803. I made his acquaintance in the Horticultural Society's garden at Chiswick, where he was placed in 1823. He was chiefly employed then in training the creepers and newly introduced plants on the walls there, which first excited my attention; and being in want of a gardener here, I asked Mr Sabine, who was then at the head of the establishment, whether he thought that young man would do? He said, 'young and untried', but spoke so favourably that I had no doubt.

The young man had made a large lake in 1822 at Sir Gregory Page-Turner's place near Woburn. He came to Chatsworth in 1826. ...

At the kitchen garden he found four pine-houses; two vineries which contained eight bunches of grapes; two good peach-houses, and a few cucumber frames. There were no houses at all for plants, and there was nowhere a plant of later introduction than about the year 1800. There were eight rhododendrons, and not one camellia. ... In a very short time a great change appeared in pleasure-ground and garden: vegetables, of which there had been none, fruit in perfection and flowers. The twelve men with brooms in their hands on the lawn began to sweep, the labourers to work with activity. The kitchen garden was so low and exposed to floods from the river, that I supposed the first wish of the new gardener would be to remove it to some other place – but he made it answer. In 1829, the management of the woods was entrusted to him, and gradually they were rescued from a prospect of destruction. Not till 1823 did I take to caring for my plants in earnest. The old greenhouse was converted into a stove, the greenhouse at the gardens was built, the Arboretum invented and formed. Then started up *Orchidaceae*, and three successive houses were built to receive their increasing numbers. In 1835 the intelligent gardener, John Gibson, was despatched to India to secure the *Amherstia nobilis*, and other treasures of the East. The colossal new Conservatory was invented and begun in 1836; the following year Baron Ludwig was so charmed with its conception that he stripped his garden at the Cape of the rarest produce of Africa.

William Spencer, 6th Duke of Devonshire
Handbook to Chatsworth and Hardwick
1844

The Spring Garden

WILLIAM ROBINSON (1838–1935) *was the creator of the wild garden, releasing plants from the formal bedding-out of the Victorian era. For much of the twentieth century, his ideas were extremely influential worldwide — though at the time when he was writing, there was furious opposition. Today, his writing seems obvious, but in 1883 it was revolutionary.*

The usual way of 'spring gardening' is 'bedding' of Forget-me-nots, Pansies, Daisies, Catchflies, and Hyacinths in beds and in ribbons; but this way of cultivating spring flowers is far too narrow, and the best is to scatter spring flowers wherever they will grow. Many country gardens are as bare and ugly in their dug borders as a London cemetery or park, while every pleasure-ground, of open space for grass with trees on it, may be made delightful with winter Aconite and Snowdrop, spring Snowflake, blue Anemone and many other flowers dotted in the grass, and under the branches of summer-leafing trees. Some little plants that flower and ripen their leaves early find a home under Beech or Oak or other deciduous trees; they complete their season's work before the leaves come on the trees, and in spring are seen happy under the branches. Wherever wild flowers grow well, numerous additions from other countries may be made to them. If we have a grove where the wood Anemone grows naturally (a common occurrence enough), nothing is easier than to associate the blue Apennine Anemone with it. A delightful addition also, if the soil be chalky, is the yellow Anemone (*A. ranunculoides*). Or does the Bluebell or wood Hyacinth grow with us? Then certainly in the same place, or near it, will also grow the bell-flowered Scilla and S. *bifolia* – not native plants, but perfectly hardy in our country. Various kinds of Daffodils or Narcissus, as, for example, the different forms of Poet's or Pheasant-eye Narcissus, will grow in any place where the common Daffodil will. The beautiful wood Forget-me-not may be sown in any wood, copse or shrubbery, and thus it may be that, apart from the garden proper, much may be done in adding the glory of spring flowers to any place where there are trees and grasses. The corners of an old orchard are delightful for experiments of this kind.

In the garden proper, we may look at the many positions in which spring flowers may be grown before we come to the 'spring bedding'. The fashion of leaving beds of Roses, choice shrubs, etc., bare of all but what might be called their proper occupants should be given up. In many places the half bare Rose beds alone would be a home for numerous beautiful spring flowers – Pansies, Violets, choice Daffodils, Scillas, and for pretty dwarf plants established in colonies between the Roses, double Primroses being particularly happy in such positions. The slight shade such plants receive in summer from the other tenants of the bed assists them, and they do better here than in bare borders. Where the Rhododendron beds are planted in an 'open' way, as they often are (and they never ought to be jammed together), we may have a garden of another delightful kind, the peat-loving plants will be quite at home there – much more so than in any bare borders. The white wood Lily of America, the Virginian Lungwort, the Canadian Bloodroot, and the various Dog's-tooth Violets enjoy peat beds. When we come to borders and beds of favourite spring flowers, such as Polyanthus, Primroses in their coloured forms, Cowslips, Auriculas, in which the self-coloured and border kinds are delightful, we can 'cut and come again' for the flowers, and they are also convenient for division and exchange. Then along favourite walks in quiet places, a rich border for those glorious Polyanthuses and coloured Primroses and any other favourite free spring flowers may be made, and so before we come to the pattern 'massing' of spring flowers we have a variety of ways of enjoying them more artistic than spring 'bedding out' pure. That may follow the fashion of the hour, and be arranged according to taste, with a considerable variety of material — Forget-me-nots, Daisies (both variegated and green), Silene, Pansy, Violet, Hyacinth, Anemone and Tulip. If we have a group of beds and, say, a parterre under a window or in any other conspicuous position, a bright and pretty effect may be formed; but even without any such thing, fair gardens of spring flowers may be made in every place. If they are so made, the problem of the design of the few formal beds of the parterre will not be so terrible.

Of late a number of beautiful forms of well-known flowers have been collected from various countries or have been raised from seed. It is believed that there now exist over a dozen different forms of the Lily-of-the-Valley, differing in size of bloom, in size of plant, and even in time of flowering. So, too, the Hepaticas, which we knew in two or three bright forms only, have broken into a much greater number. It needs only a small effort of the imagination to see what we can do with such treasures when they are sufficiently increased to be valuable for general garden decoration. Apart from these new forms of old friends, many wholly new species are being introduced yearly, thus adding to the store from which we may draw to make our spring gardens rich in form, colour and fragrance.

William Robinson
The English Flower Garden
JOHN MURRAY
1883

Rabbit's Ears and Other Delights

MRS C.W. EARLE (1836–1925) was one of those splendid Victorian ladies
who was expert in everything connected to the home. Her book, a meandering mixture
of diary, cooking and gardening hints, was put together at the request of her nieces,
who painstakingly encouraged her to share her experience and opinions.

May 22 – Not the smallest and dryest garden should be without *Stachys lanata*, a white woolly leaved plant, called Rabbit's Ears by cottage children, and particularly attractive to some people, who through life retain the love of a child for something woolly and soft. Certain characteristics are always reminding us, especially in some women, even when old, that they were once children. These leaves were formerly used as edgings to beds in a very objectionable way; but when grown in large clumps they are most useful for picking. When cut, they go on growing in water, as Buttercups and Forget-me-nots do, and mix very well with many flowers, especially with *Narcissus poeticus*, any of the German Irises, and the lovely white *Scilla campanulata*, a cheap bulb, of which we can hardly have too many. There is a blue and pink kind, but the white is the most lovely; and, in my opinion, all three are better worth growing than the usual Hyacinths, double or single. I think the people who live in the country in spring would find it more satisfactory to grow their greenhouse bulbs in large, open pans, several together, and covered with some of the mossy Saxifrages, than the usual two or three in a pot that gardeners are so fond of. If the pan has no hole at the bottom for drainage, you must put in lots of crocks, and be careful not to over-water; but bulbs like their roots moist.

I made a curious experiment with the little double Prunus. One moved last autumn, and one moved last spring out of the nursery into a sunny, sheltered border,

Venetian Fruit

Most of us lucky enough to live in Venice would not bother too much with a garden.
But FREDERICK EDEN *(1828–1916) – Gertrude Jekyll's brother-in-law and Anthony*
Eden's great-uncle – had other ideas. The Giardino Eden on the island of Giudecca
was actually the work of Caroline Eden, Jekyll's sister, while Frederick,
an invalid, would lie in its shade, surrounded by dogs.

There has been a great improvement in the fruit of Venice since we've known it, in obedience to the law of constant progress that happily prevails despite the doubts of the soured or unhappy. A pear was unknown other than the small brown native which ripened and decayed in August. Now from trees brought from Milan we gather grand fruit of the names best known in exhibitions, and eat delicious pears from July to May. The figs were prized for their size; now we have three or four kinds notable for their excellence in taste. Of grapes I write later; suffice it now to say that if not so large as those growing in English hothouses, ours will yield to none in flavour. The strawberries were of the woodland without the woods that gave them their fruit and shelter; now we have them of good size in quality, though curiously the several varieties we have imported have merged their differences and agreed to make one first-rate family. Just as English and other races have founded across the ocean that excellent human type, the American.

Raspberries will not bear our whiff of the sea, but gooseberries give us tarts when tiny, and are less crude than the fruit grown at home. When ripe in July they are neglected, for there is so much fruit that is better. Currants, white, red and black, are great bearers. Of apples on the Giudecca we only know the flower, though on the island of Sant Erasmo near by, some trees now do fairly well. Peaches are excellent. Years ago the fruit that bore the name had a hard yellow flesh that clung to its skin, and uncooked was uneatable. Now it would be difficult to find better peaches of sorts early, mid and late from July to October. Apricots are plentiful but not so very good. I suppose they ripen too quickly to get the mellow flavour of an English wall-grown apricot; and nectarines will not grow.

Plums of very many sorts are unrivalled. My youth remembers at home the joy of the greengage; the lesser pleasure of a well-ripened egg plum when you found one; and the wholesome tartness of a wine-sour tart. This last we have not. I believe out of Yorkshire it is difficult to find, but with us the sun does the cooking of kinds that are similar: the egg plum is always ripened, the greengage is a delight, and a dark sister, the black gage, dark blue without and golden green within, is in the fulness of flavour as a brunette of the south to a flaxen-coloured German. We have, too, the golden drops, each one mouthful of sun-sugared plum excellence; amoli, suchetti and many others all of merit.

Of fruit less known there are the Kaki and Nespolo that come from Japan. The last is very good in early spring; they ripen in Venice as late as May. And the Kaki is a golden bag of sugar in November and December; too sweet for me, but those that like them like them greatly. Then there are melons of many sorts and great excellence. They seem, however, to require early renewal from their parent stock. The fruit grown from the seeds that come to us from England lose in a year or two their respective characters. Even Bacirro, the great yellow melon of the Greek archipelago, has a tendency to round his long form and fatten. The Egyptian water-melon, Anguria, is much grown, but those who have crushed its red flesh like frozen snow in the desert heat would scarcely recognise the Venetian temperate produce.

Our fruit then is abundant and excellent, as it should be in a temperature where it should form, and does form, a large part of one's daily diet.

Frederick Eden
'A Garden in Venice'
Country Life
1903

Italian Villas and Their Gardens

EDITH WHARTON (1862–1937), *best known as a novelist, was passionate about gardens –*
Italian gardens especially. I make no apology for the length of her paean of praise to
them, because she unerringly puts her finger on the secrets behind their beauty.
Read her dissection of their design and you will come a long
way towards being able to copy their lines.

T hough it is an exaggeration to say that there are no flowers in Italian gardens, yet to enjoy and appreciate the Italian garden-craft one must always bear in mind that it is independent of floriculture.

The Italian garden does not exist for its flowers; its flowers exist for it: they are a late and infrequent adjunct to its beauties, a parenthetical grace counting as only one more touch in the general effect of enchantment. This is no doubt partly explained by the difficulty of cultivating any but spring flowers in so hot and dry a climate, and the result has been a wonderful development of the more permanent effects to be obtained from the three other factors in garden-composition – marble, water and perennial verdure – and the achievement, by their skilful blending, of a charm independent of the seasons.

It is hard to explain to the modern garden-lover, whose whole conception of the charm of gardens is formed of successive pictures of flower-loveliness, how this effect of enchantment can be produced by anything so dull and monotonous as a mere combination of clipped green and stone-work.

The traveller returning from Italy, with his eyes and imagination full of the ineffable Italian garden-magic, knows vaguely that the enchantment exists; that he has been under its spell, and that it is more potent, more enduring, more intoxicating to every sense than the most elaborate and glowing effects of modern horticulture; but he may not have found the key to the mystery. Is it because the sky is bluer, because the vegetation is more luxuriant? Our midsummer skies are almost as deep, our foliage is as rich, and perhaps more varied; there are, indeed, not a few resemblances between the North American summer climate and that of Italy in spring and autumn.

Some of those who have fallen under the spell are inclined to ascribe the Italian garden-magic to the effect of time; but, wonder-working as this undoubtedly is, it leaves many beauties unaccounted for. To seek the answer one must go deeper: the garden must be studied in relation to the house, and both in relation to the landscape. The garden of the Middle Ages, the garden one sees in old missal illuminations and in early woodcuts, was a mere patch of ground within the castle precincts, where 'simples' were grown around a central well-head and fruit was espaliered against the walls. But in the rapid flowering of Italian civilisation the castle walls were soon thrown down, and the garden expanded, taking in the fish-pond, the bowling-green, the rose-arbour and the clipped walk. The Italian country house, especially in the centre and the south of Italy was always built on a hillside, and one day the architect looked forth from the terrace of his villa, and saw that, in his survey of the garden, the enclosing landscape was naturally included: the two formed a part of the same composition.

The recognition of this fact was the first step in the development of the great garden-art of the Renaissance: the next was the architect's discovery of the means by which nature and art might be fused in this picture. He had now three problems to deal with: his garden must be adapted to the architectural lines of the house it adjoined; it must be adapted to the requirements of the inmates of the house, in the sense of providing shady walks, sunny bowling-greens, parterres and orchards, all conveniently accessible; and lastly it must be adapted to the landscape around it. At no time and in no country has this triple problem been so successfully dealt with as in the treatment of the Italian country house from the beginning of the sixteenth to the end of the eighteenth century; and in the blending of different elements, the subtle transition from the fixed and formal lines of art to the shifting and irregular lines of nature, and lastly in the essential convenience and livableness of the garden, lies the fundamental secret of the old garden-magic.

However much other factors may contribute to the total impression of charm, yet by eliminating them one after another, by *thinking away* the flowers, the sunlight, the rich tinting of time, one finds that, underlying all these, there is the deeper harmony of design which is independent of any adventitious effects. This does not imply that a plan of an Italian garden is as beautiful as the garden itself. The more permanent materials of which the latter is made – the stonework, the evergreen foliage, the effects of rushing or motionless water, above all the lines of the natural scenery — all form a part of the artist's design. But these things are as beautiful at one season as at another; and even these are but the accessories of the fundamental plan. The inherent beauty of the garden lies in the grouping of its parts — in the converging lines of its long ilex walks, the alternation of sunny open spaces with cool woodland shade, the proportion between terrace and bowling-green, or between the height of a wall and the width of a path. None of these details was negligible to the landscape-architect of the Renaissance: he considered the distribution of shade and sunlight, of straight lines of masonry and rippled lines of foliage, as carefully as he weighed the relation of his whole composition to the scene about it.

Then, again, anyone who studies the old Italian gardens will be struck with the way in which the architect broadened and simplified his plan if it faced a grandiose landscape. Intricacy of detail, complicated groupings of terraces, fountains, labyrinths and porticoes are found in sites where there is no great sweep of landscape attuning the eye to larger impressions. The farther north one goes, the less grand the landscape becomes and the more elaborate the garden. The great pleasure-grounds overlooking the Roman Campagna are laid out on severe and majestic lines: the parts are few; the total effect is one of breadth and simplicity.

It is because, in the modern revival of gardening, so little attention has been paid to these first principles of the art that the garden-lover should not content himself with a vague enjoyment of old Italian gardens, but should try to extract from them principles which may be applied at home. He should observe, for instance, that the old Italian garden was meant to be lived in — a use to which, at least in America, the modern garden is seldom put. He should note that, to this end, the grounds were as carefully and conveniently planned as the house, with broad paths (in which two or more could go abreast) leading from one division to another; with shade easily accessible from the house, as well as a sunny sheltered walk for winter; and with effective transitions from the dusk of wooded alleys to open flowery spaces or to the level sward of the bowling-green. He should remember that the terraces and formal gardens adjoined the house, that the ilex or laurel walks beyond were clipped into shape to effect a transition between the straight lines of masonry and the untrimmed growth of the woodlands to which they led, and that each step away from architecture was a nearer approach to nature.

The cult of the Italian garden has spread from England to America, and there is a general feeling that, by placing a marble bench here and a sun-dial there, Italian 'effects' may be achieved. The results produced, even where much money and thought have been expended, are not altogether satisfactory; and some critics have thence inferred that the Italian garden is, so to speak, *untranslatable*, that it cannot be adequately rendered in another landscape and another age.

Certain effects, those which depend on architectural grandeur as well as those due to colouring and age, are no doubt unattainable; but there is, none the less, much to be learned from the old Italian gardens, and the first lesson is that, if they are to be a real inspiration, they must be copied, not in the letter but in the spirit. That is, a marble sarcophagus and a dozen twisted columns will not make an Italian garden; but a piece of ground laid out and planted on the principles of the old garden-craft will be, not indeed an Italian garden in the literal sense, but, what is far better, *a garden as well adapted to its surroundings as were the models which inspired it.*

This is the secret to be learned from the villas of Italy; and no one who has looked at them with this object in view will be content to relapse into vague admiration of their loveliness. As Browning, in passing Cape St Vincent and Trafalgar Bay, cried out: 'Here and here did England help me: how can I help England?' – say, so the garden-lover, who longs to transfer something of the old garden-magic to his own patch of ground at home, will ask himself, in wandering under the umbrella pines of the Villa Borghese, or through the box-parterres of the Villa Lante: 'What can I bring away from here?' And the more he studies and compares, the more inevitably will the answer be: 'Not this or that amputated statue, or broken bas-relief, or fragmentary effect of any sort, but a sense of the informing spirit – an understanding of the gardener's purpose, and of the uses to which he meant his garden to be put.'

Edith Wharton
Italian Villas and Their Gardens
CENTURY
1904

26

at. Above all – drainage, drainage, drainage is essential. More alpine plants are annually lost by defective drainage than by all the other fatalities of the garden put together (of course, I am now talking to those who, like me, have to cope with a wet winter-climate; but everywhere the rule holds good). Consider the slope of the Alps, the light, sharp grit in which the plants grow. Moisture is abundant, but it drains away with unfailing rapidity. Anything like clogging by damp or stagnant humidity in the soil is certainly fatal to mountain plants. Even bog-species resent it bitterly. And no measure will go so far to ensure success as the laying of a good eight-inch bed of clinkers at the foundation of the rock-garden, before you build the erection itself. I have never had more triumph than out of compartments in the New Garden, where I took out the soil to two and a half feet, laid a drainage bed of rough (they should be rough) broken burrs; then, atop of them, clods of coarse peat, with sharp-edged lumps of limestone or sandstone, and then old, old manure, leaf-soil in abundance, peat, sand, and good fibrous loam. This sharp drainage has done wonders, I find, for the difficult species which otherwise are liable to resent our damp winters. And the rule, together with that as to goodness of soil, is one of the few dogmas that are necessary to horticultural salvation. ...

The stone everywhere is the mountain limestone of the Craven Highlands, brought straight down from the fells of Ingleborough just above us. And this I recommend as the very best that can possibly be used for the rock-garden. It is soft, extremely beautiful in colour, and becomes fretted by air and water into the most varied and wonderful shapes, of which you can make good use without following the Almond-pudding School. The rain of the hills sometimes even makes holes right through and through; and in the Old Garden I have some big boulders, lugged off the mountains, so pierced and riddled with hollows that all you have to do is to plant your plants, and there you have a miniature rock-garden ready-made, and one too that will thrive for years without attention. There is also about the weathering of these blocks a dignity and calm which somehow make them perfectly harmonious in the very best design of rock-garden building. Popular taste prefers the wilder conformations in them, stuck up on end to look like bears or old women or monsters; but the more refined, normal specimens may be used for any mass you wish to build, and will, if properly set up, weld together so as to look as if Creation had put them there exactly so.

Reginald Farrer
My Rock-Garden
EDWARD ARNOLD
1907

Clothing the Walls

Before GERTRUDE JEKYLL (1843–1932), *no designer paid any attention to cottage gardens — a naïve art form entirely disregarded. But she and her collaborator, Sir Edwin Lutyens, valued the vernacular. It was Jekyll who influenced most twentieth-century gardens with her planting schemes and reaction to the opulent gardens of the Victorians. To read her books is to understand the direction that English gardens have taken in the last hundred years.*

For my own part I like to give a house, whatever its size or style, some dominant note in wall-planting. In my own home, which is a house of the large cottage class, the prevailing wall-growths are Vines and Figs in the south and west, and in a shady northward facing court between two projecting wings, *Clematis montana* on the two cooler sides, and again a Vine upon the other. At one angle on the warmer side of the house, where the height to the eaves is not great, China Roses have been trained up, and Rosemary, which clothes the whole foot of the wall, is here encouraged to rise with them. The colour of the China Rose bloom and the dusky green of the Rosemary are always to me one of the most charming combinations. In remembrance of the cottage example ... there is *Pyrus japonica* under the long sitting-room window. I remember another cottage that had a porch covered with the golden balls of *Kerria japonica*, and China Roses reaching up the greater part of the low walls of half timber and plastering; the pink Roses seeming to ask one which of them were the loveliest in colour; whether it was those that came against the silver-grey of the old oak or those that rested on the warm-white plaster. It should be remembered that of all Roses the pink China is the one that is more constantly in bloom than any other, for its first flowers are perfected before the end of May, and in sheltered places the later ones last till Christmas.

The *Clematis montana* in the court riots over the wall facing east and up over the edge of the roof. At least it appears to riot, but is really trained and regulated; the training favouring its natural way of throwing down streamers and garlands of its long bloom-laden cordage. At one point it runs through and over a Guelder Rose that is its only wall companion. Then it turns to the left and is trained in garlands along a moulded oak beam that forms the base of a timbered wall with plastered panels.

But this is only one way of using this lovely climbing plant. Placed at the foot of any ragged tree – old worn-out Apple or branching Thorn – or a rough brake of Bramble and other wild bushes, it will soon fill or cover it with its graceful growth and bounteous bloom. It will rush up a tall Holly or clothe an old hedgerow where thorns have run up and become thin and gappy, or cover any unsightly sheds or any kind of outbuilding. All Clematises prefer a chalky soil, but *montana* does not insist on this, and in my pictures they are growing in sandy ground. In the end of May it comes into bloom, and is at its best in the early days of June. When the flowers are going over and the white petals show that slightly shrivelled surface that comes before they fall, they give off a sweet scent like vanilla. This cannot be always smelt from the actual flowers, but it is carried by the air blowing over the flowering mass; it is a thing that is often a puzzle to owners of gardens some time in the second week of June.

Another of these Clematises, which, like the *montana* of gardens, is very near the wild species and is good for all the same purposes, is C. *flammula*, blooming in September. Very slightly trained it takes the form of flowery clouds. We show it used in various ways, on a cottage, on an oak-paled fence and on a wall combined with the feathery foliage of *Spiraea lindleyana*. I do not think there is any incident in my garden that has been more favourably noticed than the happy growth of these two plants together. The wall faces north a little west, and every year it is a delight to see not only the beauty of associated form, but the loveliness of the colouring; for the Clematis bloom has the warm white of foam and the Spiraea has leaves of a rather pale green of Lady Fern, besides a graceful fern-like form and a slight twist or turn also of a fern-like character. But this Clematis has many other uses, for bowers, arches and pergolas, as well as for many varied aspects of wild gardening.

Gertrude Jekyll
'Colour Schemes for the Flower Garden'
Country Life
1908

On Water

SIR GEORGE SITWELL (1860–1943) writes from experience: his fine garden,
still thriving at Renishaw in the north of England, distils his love of Italianate formality.
He spent years studying Italian gardens, and the small book from which this extract
is taken, ESSAY ON THE MAKING OF GARDENS, notes what he observed.
In his introduction to the book, Sitwell's son, the writer Osbert, is not entirely kind about
his father's work, as this quotation shows: 'My father was meditating, just before the hour
when the garden was to be closed, at the very bottom of the layout of Villa d'Este, between
the giant cypresses. He was deep in thought, when four ancient custodi advanced on him
from the four different quarters of the compass. Immediately, concluding the old men were
brigands (for he lived always a hundred years before his time), he, as Henry [his servant
Henry Moat] put it, "fair biffed 'em with his umbrella. You could hear 'em squawk
half a mile away!" But from such escapades, for which, alone of living men, he
seemed qualified, he always emerged victorious and scot-free. It was enough
in those days for Henry to explain that his was an English signore.'

In water the two pictures always contend, reflection and transparency being in inverse ratio to each other, and in some positions it may be better to abandon the surface and cultivate the beauties of the underworld. With a fountain basin, sculpture must necessarily be above the water, but in dealing with a still reservoir no such law is imposed upon us. We may have a merman's pool, fringed with floating lilies, where below the water-film are sea-maidens and gold-red fish and under-water palaces, and that strange power the eye has of clearing away reflection by the change to a longer focus will enhance the effect by a sudden thrill of surprise. Columns and opposing mirrors may give endless vistas of pillared halls, and if the pool is near the upper edge of a cliff a strange light may be thrown into it through an opening protected by glass. We may build up a dark screen of masonry behind it and illuminate it through a water passage from a pool beyond, or make the still more interesting experiment of 'total internal reflection', admitting the sun's rays in the later afternoon between the stems of a great hedge of beech or ilex at such an angle that the returning rays will lie along or actually under the surface of the water. Some of these will appear to be bizarre suggestions, and indeed it is likely enough that, except in great conservatories or winter gardens, under-water mirrors may produce an unquiet effect.

But until such experiments have been tried, an opinion is of little value. There are no rules in art which some great artist has not shown us how to break with advantage, and every new adventure is a voyage of discovery, the outcome of which no man may foresee. Nature has 'thousands of exquisite effects of light which are absolutely inexplicable', which can be believed only while they are seen, and by good fortune we may reap a larger harvest than we have sown.

Elsewhere the designer may prefer to play with the colour of water, seeking to reproduce those lovely hues of blue and green which the Italians of an earlier age caught and fixed in garden reservoirs, and even in small fountain basins. Water absorbs the red rays of the spectrum and is therefore a blue transparent medium, its colour when distilled being a tint of Prussian blue, as may be seen in the pure ice of the glacier crevasses. All that is necessary to bring out the natural beauty of the element by transmitted light is, firstly, a flood of strong sunshine; secondly, to look down from above as nearly vertically as possible; thirdly, to cut off reflections of the sky by trees or hedges or other dark objects. Suspended particles of glacier dust or chalk or lime add much to the brilliance of the effect, and in a country where the stone is red or yellow should give a tint of green or purple or violet. In England one may sometimes see blue or green pools at the bottom of a deserted stone-quarry: if experiments should show that good colour is unattainable at a higher level under these grey skies we shall be justified in helping it out by the use of coloured tiles.

Sir George Sitwell
Essay on the Making of Gardens
JOHN MURRAY
1909

The Right Rock

Rock gardens, long out of date, are starting to return to fashion. F.W. MEYER (died 1906), published posthumously at the turn of the twentieth century, was making his views known at the height of such gardens' popularity. However dated, his scathing (not to say snobbish) view that rockeries should look like natural features is as valid now as it was then.

The question of stones is important in the making of rock gardens, and much depends on a good selection. To use two or three different kinds for the same work – as is often done – is, I consider, a great mistake. There is no reason why rock gardens made of different materials should not occupy different parts of the garden, if it be sufficiently large. For instance, we may have a limestone rockery in one part and, say, a granite rockwork in another, but to mix them is not advisable, as it would be unnatural. To my mind, the most unsuitable of all kinds of stones for rock building are bits of glaring white spar or other gaudy stones covered with glassy crystals or of a general vitreous appearance. Owners of quarries generally put aside these pieces and sell them to would-be rock builders under the name of 'fancy rockery'. For convenience of easy handling these stones are generally broken up into pieces of almost uniform size, i.e. about one foot to two feet in length. For a collection of minerals these pretty crystals may well be enough, but they should never be used for rock building except perhaps when crushed or broken into small fragments to mix with the soil for such alpines as love a gritty medium to grow in. They are the delight of such masons and jobbing gardeners whose ideas of rock building can never advance beyond the pudding-shaped heaps of soil studded all over and at regular intervals with these uniform bits of glaring spar or crystals. Such creations may still find admirers in the shape of amateurs without horticultural knowledge, whose only garden is a tiny plot in front of a small villa. But to people whose taste has been refined by the study of Nature, the 'loud' appearance of such stones is vulgar. Why? Because it is unnatural. In Nature we may find such material in the interior of caves or in hidden crevices but never on the surface. And as we are – or should be – imitating Nature when building artificial rocks, the beauty of our garden must, under all circumstances, depend on its appearing true to Nature, the artistic grouping and blending of rocks and plants, and the picturesque effect of the whole, but never should it depend on the gorgeous colouring or staring crystals of individual stones.

The Late F.W. Meyer, edited by E.T. Cook
Rock and Water Gardens
COUNTRY LIFE
1910

Bean on Oaks

W.J. BEAN (1863–1947), *a former director of the Royal Botanic Gardens, Kew,
wrote the bible of tree-growing in Britain. His three-volume book is a marvel of clear
description allied to a lyrical appreciation of great trees. And what more worth his time
than the oak tree? He does not disappoint. If you have enough land, it's worth picking
up acorns from particularly fine oaks and raising new trees from them, as he suggests.*

Quercus: a large genus of evergreen and deciduous trees and shrubs, of which nearly three hundred species are known. Sixty to seventy are in cultivation. Leaves alternate, a spiral of five making one circuit of the branchelet, frequently lobed somewhat deeply, but occasionally merely toothed or even entire. The down on the leaves, etc., is mostly stellate. Male and female flowers occur on the same trees, but on separate inflorescences. The males are numerous on pendulous (rarely erect) catkins, small, green or greenish, forming sometimes tassel-like clusters; females few and quite inconspicuous. The most distinctive feature of the oak is its fruit, which consists of a usually egg-shaped or rounded nut (acorn), the lower part of which is more or less enclosed by a cup covered with woody, sometimes fringe-like scales. The acorn frequently takes two seasons to mature. The nearest allies of the oaks are the sweet chestnuts, beeches and hazels. One group – *Pasania* – to which *densiflora* and *cuspidata* belong, is sometimes kept apart as a distinct genus.

The oaks are amongst the finest of the large trees of temperate regions. The two native of Britain, *Q. pedunculata* and *Q. sessiflora*, are the largest and longest lived of our deciduous trees, and produce the most valuable timber. Nor are they surpassed in rugged beauty and strength. Their maximum duration of life is probably not less than one thousand years. For some reason the planting of oaks in parks and gardens has fallen into desuetude in recent times. Beyond a few coloured or variegated sorts they are now stocked by very few nurserymen, who cannot, of course, be expected to keep up supplies for which there is no demand. Few firms appear now to grow oaks in such number and variety as did Lee of Isleworth, Smith of Worcester, or Booth of Hamburg, sixty to eighty years ago. The finest collections today, after that at Kew, are Lord Ducie's at Tortworth, and the one at Aldenham got together by Mr Vicary Gibbs. To those who contemplate planting oaks I would recommend the following as a selection of twenty of the best, apart from our British species and their varieties.

DECIDUOUS *castanaefolia, Cerris, *coccinea, *conferta, imbricaria, *Leana, Libani, Lucombeana, *macranthera, *Mirbeckii, palustris, Phellos, *rubra, Toza and *velutina.

EVERGREEN Acuta, coccifera, densiflora, Ilex, phillyreoides.

Some of the deciduous species, like those marked *, are amongst the handsomest and most striking in foliage of all our big trees, and would impart distinction to any demesne, whilst *coccinea* and *palustris* give the richest touches of crimson to our autumn landscape. Q. Ilex forms a class by itself among evergreen trees hardy with us. Oaks, as a whole, thrive best on good deep loams. The old conception that the value of a soil for agriculture was indicated by the size and quality of the oaks upon it has many times been verified, not only in this country but in others, especially by the early settlers in both the east and west coast regions of N. America. Oaks should always if possible be raised from acorns, which should be kept from getting dry after gathering until sown. Grafting has, perforce, to be resorted to for special varieties and rare species; but although one may see occasionally fine grafted specimens, the practice should only be adopted where absolutely necessary, for it tends to shorten the life of the tree, and in the end retard its growth. I strongly advocate getting all oaks into their permanent places as soon as possible. If I could, I would sow all acorns in situ, for thereby the tap-root is preserved and the plant never checked, but for many reasons that is not often possible except in pure forestry. Few trees in nurseries need transplanting with greater regularity every two or three years than oaks do if their final removal is to be accomplished safely, and few suffer more through shifting if their roots have been allowed to wander at will for a longer term. Evergreen species are especially likely to die. They should never be transplanted until after they show signs of growth in late May or early June, or else in September.

W.J. Bean
Trees and Shrubs Hardy in the British Isles
JOHN MURRAY
1914

How to Move a Tree

NATHANIEL LLOYD (1867–1933), *like his more famous son,*
Christopher (see pp. 68–71), gardened at Great Dixter in East Sussex. Lloyd's
book GARDEN CRAFTSMANSHIP IN YEW AND BOX *is still the bible for topiarists.*
While there may be more modern methods for moving large trees, the technique he describes
here is ideal in tight spaces or where there is plenty of manpower but few machines.

Large trees may be moved successfully, but the degree of such success will depend much upon how large a ball of earth is retained round the roots and upon how short a time elapses before replanting. Trees which with their ball of earth weigh up to 8 cwt., may be raised and moved by half a dozen men. The ball of roots and earth should be about 4 ft across and 2½ ft deep; by the time it is moved the latter measurement will have been reduced to 2 ft by crumbling away of earth. The soil must be damp throughout. If dry, it will not hold together; if too wet, it will be greasy and sticky, so as to be almost impossible to work. All roots for 2 ft around the tree and more than 2½ ft under the surface of the ground should be cut away, including any tap root. The ground should be opened for several feet round, as necessitated by the situation, so that men engaged may work conveniently. Any long branches should be raised and tied up close to the trunk. A piece of strong canvas, such as is used by furniture removers, 15 ft square, is inserted under the ball. This is done by pulling the tree over on its side, folding and pushing the canvas as far under as possible (as a nurse puts a sheet under a patient who cannot leave bed) and then rocking the tree in the opposite direction, which will enable the canvas to be drawn still further under. This process is repeated (if necessary) until the ball of earth and roots stands in the middle of the canvas. The canvas is then drawn up to the trunk and tied securely so that the four corners form four large ears, which will afford good handles of which the men may take hold. The tree is then rocked on one side and earth thrown under and rammed tightly. On this rammed earth the tree is rocked to the other side, further earth thrown in where it was lying and rammed hard. The process is repeated until the canvas ball has been raised nearly to the original ground level, when it can be rocked, pushed and lifted on to planks, along which it can be pushed with levers and pulled by the canvas ears. At the end of the planks or under them, as may be most convenient, a Samson trolley may be brought and the ball slid or dropped on to this. Then it can be wheeled on planks used as rails to its new position, where it may be slid into the hole prepared for it and, by rocking from side to side, the canvas be folded and withdrawn in the same way as it was got under. It will be found that six or seven men are as many as can work together round the ball, which limits the size of the tree and ball which can be handled without special appliances. The new site for the tree should be drained and prepared as for hedges. The tree should be firmly staked and secured for many years after removal, until it has made fresh, strong roots that will enable it to withstand a severe gale. Such root development may be encouraged by digging deeply and wide about the new site and ramming the ground firmly after planting. It must be remembered that (except, perhaps, standing in water) nothing is so trying to a moved tree as continual strain upon its unconsolidated roots. The bigger and taller the tree and the more exposed the situation, the greater such strain may be.

Nathaniel Lloyd
Garden Craftsmanship in Yew and Box
ERNEST BENN
1925

My Perfect Vegetable Garden

The famous flower arranger of the mid-twentieth century, CONSTANCE SPRY
(1886–1960), writes longingly of her ideal vegetable garden in the dark days of the
Second World War. Her eye for interesting foliage and form is as acute with vegetables
as with flowers. Indeed, her championship of plantings of artichokes, fennel
and red kale pre-dates similar arrangements by Sir Terence Conran
and other garden designers by fifty-odd years.

On this first day of January I will tell you what, in even an indifferent plot, gives pleasure. There is a splash of bright green like a rug thrown on the brown earth lying next to rows of grey flags, just common or garden parsley

and leeks. There's a breadth of what might be grey-green tropical fern, but is, in fact, chou de Russie. There's grandeur and colour in rows of red cabbage and the purple decorative kale.

There are scoffers who find truly comic eccentricity in the consideration of beauty in what they call common vegetables. These are suffering from blindness caused by familiarity. Even the most hilarious mocker would have been compelled to stop laughing to admire a certain long border of dark green curly kale that I saw lately in a grey-walled garden. I came on it suddenly and stopped dead; the plants were more imposing than Victorian funeral plumes, and as covered with delicate bloom as a bunch of hothouse grapes. The bloom and curl of the leaves gave an illusion of softest velvet.

Every one who has a garden knows of something that looks good. Your eye can be arrested by a row of beans on an allotment, because the bean poles have been well and symmetrically set. Sweet corn can look like tropical bedding, globe artichokes are as fine in form as the classic acanthus.

Gradually I am gathering together these mental pictures, and one day the kaleidoscope will set into a bright symmetrical figure, and I shall have the pattern of a new kitchen garden. For I am only waiting for the war to be over to make myself the sort of kitchen garden I've always wanted. ...

Symmetry and formality will be the keynote. In a patterned order I want straight and intersecting paths, formal edgings, rectangular beds, long lines of plants like an illustration in a Dutch bulb catalogue, and, over the whole, a green-grey bloom jewelled at intervals with rubied fruits, with here and there an embroidery of strawberries. ...

I used to like flower borders in the kitchen garden, but each year I become more and more in favour of edgings of herbs, backed, perhaps, with lower-growing vegetables.

By using the gold and silver thymes, dwarf lavender, winter and summer savory, basil, marjoram, parsley and chives, good contrasts of green, grey, and gold may be contrived. In winter some of the green remains to give a sense of life; in summer this is chequered with subdued colour of the flowers and the whole drowsy with the noise of bees.

A wide border of vegetables may be broken into bays by using low dividing hedges of the common fennel. I have had such a hedge for two or three years: about three foot high, thick, soft feathery green all through the summer until, in autumn, it flung itself up into shapes and stately yellow flower. Smooth, glaucous stems, filmy leaves, clean angles at the joints, and delicacy combined with strength are qualities in this plant.

And now the walls. I harp on the walls because I want them so much. They will be patterned geometrically with espalier fruits. They ought, of course, to have those delightful little thatched eaves that gave such quality to walled gardens in those days when time really was on our side – and, as I am being so entirely unrestrained in saying what I want, I think I'll add that one wall at least will have niches at intervals down its entire length as they are in Charles Bury's garden in Co. Meath.

Constance Spry
Come into the Garden, Cook
J.M. DENT
1942

Think of Thyme

VITA SACKVILLE-WEST (1892–1962), *one of the most celebrated gardeners
in the world, wrote a column in* THE OBSERVER *newspaper during the 1940s and
1950s, long before her garden at Sissinghurst in the south of England became famous.
In the column she passed on advice, admitted failures and asked for help.
As this extract from Vita's anthologized version of the column,* IN YOUR GARDEN,
shows, it is still as inspiring as when it was first written.

JUNE 18, 1950

Two years ago I had what I thought might be a bright idea. It has turned out so bright, in both senses of the word, that I must pass it on. I had two small windswept beds (the size was eight yards long by five yards wide each) divided by a path of paving stones down the middle. I tried every sort of thing in them, including a mad venture of hollyhocks, which, of course, got flattened by the prevailing south-west wind, however strongly we staked them. So then I decided I must have something very low-growing, which would not suffer from the wind, and scrapped the hollyhocks, and dibbled in lots and lots of thyme, and now have a sort of lawn which, while it is densely flowering in purple and red, looks like a Persian carpet laid flat on the ground out of doors. The bees think that I have laid it for their especial benefit. It really is a lovely sight; I do not want to boast, but I cannot help being pleased with it; it is so seldom that one's experiments in gardening are wholly successful.

The thyme we used was the cultivated or garden form of the wild thyme, *Thymus serpyllum*, in fact the form you see creeping about between paving stones on paths and terraces. *Serpyllum* comes from the Latin *serpere*, to creep; think of serpent; and in fact two old English names for the wild thyme were serpille and serpolet. My serpolet lawn. ... The Romans believed its fragrance to be a remedy for melancholia; and in later years, our own Elizabethan times, it was thought to cure sciatica and whooping cough, headache, phrenzy, and lethargy.

We had the common purple sort, and the sort called *coccineus* to give the redder patches, and also a little of the white, which varied the pattern.

I have planted a few bulbs of small things in amongst the thyme, to give some interest in the spring, when the thyme is merely green. A patch of crocuses; a patch of the miniature narcissus; a patch of the little pink cyclamen. It occurs to me also that if you have not a flat bed to devote to a thyme-lawn you could fill a sunny bank with it. Steep grass banks are always awkward to mow, but the thyme would not need any mowing, and it should revel in a sunny exposure with the good drainage of a slope. You might plant some of the rock-roses, or sun roses, hybrids of *Helianthemum vulgare*, amongst the thyme on a bank, though I would not do so in a thyme-lawn, where it would spoil the effect of flatness. These sun-roses can be obtained in a variety of brilliant colours, ranging from pale buff and yellow to tomato pink and deep red, and they flower for at least six weeks during May and June.

Vita Sackville-West
In Your Garden
MICHAEL JOSEPH
1951

The Case for Willows

It's surprising how many nurserymen become lyrical about the plants
they propagate. If you specialize in plants, it does, of course, require true love, but
WALTER INGWERSEN (1885–1960) *writes about them almost as though*
they were pets. His is the perfect book for those who want
to plant a true garden of native British plants.

The willows [belong] ... to a very ancient genus indeed. They covered much of the northern world at the time when great glaciers spread over much of Europe, Asia and America. As the climate became milder and the ice retreated, some of these little Willows were left stranded upon our higher mountain-tops and our northern moors, and there they have survived to the present day.

To this day the last tree life, as you go to the North Pole, is one of these little Willows, only an inch or two high, but with a vast root system in the few upper inches of ground that are not permanently frozen. Bearing in mind that these northern dwarfs have to support for nine months of the year the great weight of many feet deep of snow and that their active growing season is restricted to often less than three months, they have little enough time to produce their catkin flowers and a few leaves and possibly a fraction of an inch of woody growth before winter closes down on them. Thus their annual increase in size can only be measured in decimals. Being, as I have stated, of very ancient lineage, they keep firmly and resolutely to the family tradition and remain the true gnarled dwarfs even when transplanted to gardens in climates where they can grow, if they would, for nine months of the year. I love them for this steadfastness and have collected them for many years, until at one time I had about fifty different species in my garden. Great Britain does not give us so many, but six or possibly seven good species are to be found and may legitimately find admission to our specialised garden, where, indeed, places of honour should be found for them in choice nooks and cool corners of the rock garden and possibly in the best part of our little boggy corner.

The best known of these dwarf Willows is *Salix repens*, the Creeping Willow. It is to be found on heaths, moors and in sandy places as far south as Ashdown Forest in Sussex. There it forms low, straggling shrubs with stems that creep far underneath the ground and send up loose tangles of branches about a foot high. Its leaves are narrow and oblong and generally less than an inch long. Male and female catkins are borne on different plants, and the male plants are especially delightful when studded with tiny silky and silvery pussy Willows. Both stems and leaves are covered with silky down whilst they are young, and there is a handsome variety, S. repens argentea, in which this silvery down persists until leaf fall. The female catkins are not showy until the seeds open and each seed displays the silky parachute with which nature provides it. Despite this free production of seeds with their ready means for disposal, I have yet to find self-sown seedlings of this species. In the garden, in richer soil, this one southern dwarf Willow may show an inclination to grow and spread farther than is desirable, but it is easily cut back to the desired dimensions.

S. lapponum, the Downy Willow, does not come farther south than Scotland, and even there must be looked for in the mountains. It varies a good deal in stature and in the size of its leaves, but it rarely makes bushes more than 2 or 3 feet high. These bushes may spread into a much-branched scrubby bush with oblong or lanceolate leaves covered above and below with cottony down, especially so early in the year. By the autumn the leaves may be nearly glabrous. This Willow does not creep underground, and has much larger catkins which may be an inch long when in full bloom. This would make a good background shrub for the heath or rock garden. It is the tallest of these dwarf Willows that I would admit to our garden.

S. lanata is the Woolly Willow and greatly beloved by my family and me, especially in the early spring when it bears its handsome big catkins covered with a silky fur of lovely golden yellow. It looks as if dozens of young fluffy canaries were perched all over its gnarled branches. This Willow can, in the course of years, become a stoutish, much-branched shrub 2 feet high and 4 to 5 feet in diameter. It is widely spread in Arctic and northern regions, and in Britain it is only found in a few rocky glens in Scotland. It likes a cool spot, moist by preference, and it likes some good porous lumps of sandstone to rest its branches on and to keep its roots under. You will find it a slow grower and you will have to start with young plants; but it will soon reach the stage where it brings a few catkins each spring, and the bush will improve from year to year and ultimately make a fine specimen plant for you. Its leaves are roundish and covered with soft, silky wool, and even the younger branches have this silvery-grey woolly covering. The side of a little pool in the rock garden or a little rocky island in the garden pond are ideal positions for so striking and lovely a plant, which draws everybody's attention, even during the leafless winter stage.

S. Sadleri (Syme) is either a very much smaller form of the Woolly Willow or possibly a hybrid of it. It has been suggested that *S. myrsinites*, the Whortle Willow, might be the other parent of this. It is excessively rare and has so far been found in only one spot in the mountains of Forfar. Several of our better nurseries have propagated this from cuttings and are able to supply young plants. If your garden is very small, I suggest that *S. Sadleri* should be planted instead of *S. lanata*.

Where several of these Willows grow in close proximity the pollen, wind-borne or carried by bees, results in several very interesting natural hybrids, which will increase the number of these pleasant little shrubs for our garden.

Walter E.T. Ingwersen
Wild Flowers in the Garden
GEOFFREY BLES
1951

Enough to Puzzle a Monkey

*In this extract GEOFFREY GRIGSON (1905–1985), poet, botanist, plant-hunter
(and husband of English cookery writer Jane), makes a plea for the revival of
the monkey-puzzle tree, planted in groves. More seriously, he would like
gardeners not to cut down trees that just might be endangered.*

A*raucaria araucana* was discovered late in the eighteenth century by a Spaniard searching the Chilean mountains for a good naval timber. The seeds bestowed 'a great boon on the poor Indians which nothing but a small parrot divides with them'. Boiled and dried, they were to be had before long in the market at Valparaiso. When George Vancouver made his expedition across the Pacific, he took with him the Scottish plant collector, Archibald Menzies, of Aberfeldy. In Valparaiso, so the story goes, Menzies dined with the Spanish viceroy and pocketed some of the monkey-puzzle seeds from the viceroy's table. Then on the voyage home he raised a number of plants on the ship, which reached London in the autumn of 1795. ... Like many other introductions, the monkey puzzle was thought at first to be tender; and seeds had to be imported and larger stocks raised before it became fashionable. In 1838, in Scotland, a young tree, a foot to a foot and a half tall, or short, would have cost you three guineas. In 1834 a Cornish baronet purchased a well-grown tree for twenty-five pounds which was planted in his garden at Pencarrow. This monkey puzzle deserves celebration. The baronet's guests stood around while the tree was being planted. One of them, the parliamentary lawyer, Charles Austin (1799–1834) pricked himself on the leaves and exclaimed, 'It would be a puzzle to a monkey.' So the monkey puzzle was christened. But not many people were going to buy seedlings at three guineas apiece, or larger trees for twenty-five pounds. Veitch of Exeter [Devon], one of the great firms of English nurserymen, sent the Cornishman William Lobb to make collections in South America. In 1844 Lobb sent home a consignment of monkey-puzzle seeds. ...

The noble monkey puzzle we had in our garden was planted before 1850 and I am pretty certain it came from Veitch's at Exeter, which was only fifty miles away; in which case it must have been grown from William Lobb's consignment. Lobb, by the way, also sent home, not the first but the second consignment of seeds, of the giant sequoia. This was in 1855 and one of these, as well, may have grown into the vicarage-garden tree which was so useful to the goldcrests. I was not, I am afraid, altogether kind to that monkey puzzle in return for the delight it gave me by way of its seeds, its appearance, and the dead branches which made such excellent scimitars after the leaves fell off, when I was reading *The Arabian Nights*. I wounded it to investigate the sap, such being my herbalistic mind. It oozed out milky and aromatic. I should have been glad to know that Chileans applied the sap to cure 'the most violent rheumatic headaches'.

Araucaria araucana has become rare in the wild. There are perhaps more monkey puzzles flourishing in our oceanic climate, comfily domesticated, than there are wild ones on the lower Andean slopes. Wild horses are extinct and the horse continues only on the bounty and in the protection of men. So it may be with the monkey puzzle, so long as we do not reject it. Reaction, change in fashion, did bring it into danger thirty years ago, and we do not see it so often as a newly planted tree. Yet feeling now is perhaps for it, and not against it. The vicarage tree was cut down, though not in my family's time;

but I am glad to say it has thrown up a new youngster from the roots. Gardeners, as a last word on the monkey puzzle, might use it with more imagination. Maybe it is best of all as a single tree surrounded with grass; but monkey puzzles do make a delightful grove if you have them of different ages and heights. I noticed such a grove, in which the trees looked like giant bedding-out plants, at the head of the millionaires' row, the Avenue Louise, in Brussels. Brussels is a bit dry for Araucarias, so they looked somewhat drab, dark, and unhealthy, but the arrangement of them was perfect.

Geoffrey Grigson
Gardenage or The Plants of Ninhursaga
ROUTLEDGE & KEGAN PAUL
1952

Lupins

I find it delightful to think that, according to this account by E.R. JANES,
one stubborn old gent from England's north country (where they specialize in stubborn old gents) took on the world's plant-breeders from his allotment. How they laughed at his attempts at breeding a new kind of lupin — bigger, better all round — until he did. The Russell lupin still leads the world.

In the north country a worker named George Russell made lupin breeding his hobby. He had a small garden and allotment in which he only grew lupins. He had little scientific knowledge, and relied mainly on acute observation and perhaps a little luck. Fortunately for him and the gardening world *Lupinus polyphyllus* crosses readily with other *Lupinus* species, and Russell procured a wide range of species, cultivated them in his garden and proceeded to cross them, if not indiscriminately at least very haphazardly.

He did so for many years. Most people laughed at him, and the results were meagre until one day he announced that he had bred a new race. Out of all the experiments, varieties had appeared with broad spikes, many flowers on each spike and each flower a particularly fine one. Instead of the narrow pointed keel and meagre standards, lupins now had generous fat keels, large wings and upstanding standards with a breadth which made them very much more striking than any lupins previously known. Yet few people were impressed. Several plant distributors were asked to see the new lupins, but most of them, though faintly interested, thought them of little value. But old George Russell persisted, and finally they were taken up by a well-known firm and distributed to every temperate part of the world where lupins could be grown. These, and the varieties which followed soon, ousted all the older varieties and gave promise of many striking varieties to come.

E.R. Janes
The Flower Garden
PENGUIN
1952

The Joy of Compost

MARGERY FISH (1888–1969) *was married to Walter, editor of the* DAILY MAIL *newspaper in London and a man accustomed to being in command. Together, they set out to create a garden at East Lambrook Manor in Somerset. Margery was by far the better gardener but, until Walter died, she had to obey his brusque orders.*

All this time we were doing our best to improve our terrible clay. We had endless bonfires and Walter tried so hard to get me to take the ash for the garden before rain had had a chance to wash some of the goodness into the soil. I wouldn't admit the necessity. There was always something else more important I wanted to do and it was often a week before I trundled it off to my flower beds. Now, of course, I am as fervent a disciple as Walter ever was. All the wood ash from my open fires is shared among the plants that particularly like potash, magnolias and irises particularly, and I give some to the raspberries, and in the winter the apple trees get

their share. When I grew potatoes and tomatoes they, too, were lucky. To distribute it evenly throughout the rest of the garden I now incorporate it in my compost.

Everyone has a theory about composting. I got my recipe from an American book, and I find it works out well. All green stuff is put in a heap to rot down. Perennial weeds and evergreen material are not used, but everything else, including kitchen refuse, grass cuttings, great mountains of nepeta, aubrietia, Michaelmas daisies and all other herbaceous things that are cut down. For the kitchen refuse I keep a big brown pot (commonly known as 'the gash') on the window sill behind the sink, and into it go all the tea-leaves, apple peels, onion skins and coffee grounds. Also crushed egg shells. Walter made a great fuss about egg shells, he disliked them so and contended that it was silly to bother about them when I could get all the lime I wanted for a few pence. But I think my plants enjoy a mixed diet and I would not deny them little tit-bits of shell, but I did see that they were crushed very finely so that they did not intrude too forcibly on my lord's eye. I noticed great mounds of coffee grounds at Kew, so I know I am on firm ground there, and as for tea-leaves, you have only to see what emptying the tea does to a wilting plant. I have known trees and shrubs brought back from the dead by having tea and tea-leaves administered to them after every meal, and I am sure one reason why Madonna lilies thrive in cottage gardens and not in ours is because they get tea and washing-up water and all manner of good things given to them. I don't like the messiness of tea-leaves thrown on the flower beds, but I use them and the tea that is left in the teapot in the compost. The liquid is particularly good, in fact a necessity, for in very dry weather the compost needs generous watering to speed decay.

I leave this heap until it is quite brown, and then I combine it with other ingredients to stand again. How long one leaves it depends on the speed of decomposition and the supply of material. I have now built up such reserves that the making of the final heap is done in the winter, and the following autumn I have a plentiful supply of super nourishment with which to enrich the garden.

My final heap is made in four layers, repeated until all the material is used up. First there is a generous layer of my rotted compost, then an equal depth of farmyard manure. This is then covered with earth and thickly dosed with wood ash. Pipes are inserted vertically at regular intervals down the heap as it is being built, so that it shall be ventilated. I like to use very young manure so that a high temperature kills any weed seeds that may be lurking in the compost. As my natural soil is clay, and such heavy clay that it doesn't change a bit during its year's sojourn in the heap but comes out a soggy solid mass, like a layer of marzipan in an Easter cake, I am now using sand instead of soil in the heap, but finish with grass tufts skimmed from the vegetable garden. These turned upside down seal the heap and keep in the heat to do its work thoroughly. Very old sawdust can be used instead of sand but it must be well weathered.

No one can call a compost heap beautiful so I hide mine in a discreet little hedged enclosure – our old friend *Lonicera nitida* again. Another enclosure beyond hides a deep pit where I pile oak and beech leaves for leaf mould, a heap of peat mould and the manure heap.

As a lot of the goodness must seep into the ground from my compost heaps, I have had the bottom of the compost enclosure concreted. Instead of having the ground quite level it slopes down very slightly, and along the lower side I have about a foot of vertical concrete (breeze blocks in fact). My compost enclosures are at the top of a ditch, so it has been easy for me to run out three small drains into the ditch. The rich ooze from the heaps drains into receptacles placed to receive it and gives me a constant supply of liquid manure. It is wonderful what a fillip this diluted good water gives to a plant that is just coming into flower. In the summer the sweet corn particularly is the lucky recipient of this largesse.

There is a theory that if compost is made on a concrete base one will be deprived of the worms which would normally come up from the soil. I don't know where the worms come from but my heap is always full of very lively, very pink worms, so I haven't lost these busy little underground workers by working on a clean foundation.

Margery Fish
We Made a Garden
W.H. & L. COLLINGRIDGE LIMITED
1956

A Rose for Every Taste

GRAHAM STUART THOMAS (1909–2003) *was loaded down with gardening honours:*
the Victoria Medal of Honour, the Veitch Memorial Medal and the Dean Hole Medal.
He was awarded the OBE for his work with the National Trust in England and Wales.
But to most of us he is the man who made us re-evaluate old-fashioned roses.
In this extract, he describes how to plant old roses and their companions.

The coming of the rose is to me the very crown of the year. From the first delicate-flowered pale yellow species and Scots Roses that open, in company with the Cherokee and Banksian Roses, on warm wall, to the last poignant autumn blooms, the rose gives unequalled beauty. There is a rose for every taste. Whether we are newly awakened to flowers and delight in the dazzling display of Floribundas, or the more exquisite blooms of the classy Hybrid Teas, or whether our senses have developed still further and embrace the perfect roses of a more refined and elegant age; or whether we go back to the exquisite grace and charm of the original species, there is, I repeat, a rose for every taste.

Roses have so much 'fullness' about them; they are full of vigour if the most suitable kinds are planted and reasonably trained; they are full of contrast, their rounded flowers, sprinkled over the network of leaves, create a delightful effect; they are often full of petals, of a good texture of rich velvet or of shining silk; and they are full of scent. They are rich throughout in qualities which have been favourites with gardeners of all ages. Listen to M. Cochet-Cochet: 'Le Rosier est beaucoup le plus important de tous les arbustes cultivés pour l'ornement des jardins.'

This paean of praise from a worthy French nurseryman may perhaps require a little qualification. Roses are certainly the favourite flowering shrubby plants of today, but with few exceptions they cannot form the framework of a garden. Evergreens are needed for such positions. Roses are more suitable for foreground colour-work, the filling-in of bays between heavier material, the covering of stumps, hedgerows, and banks with their long trails, and for growing near to the eye and nose, that their beauties may easily reach the senses. Apart from their loss of leaves in winter the Rugosa

Roses and the new hybrid 'Nevada' are flowering shrubs of the heaviest calibre, and can be used in important positions governing the design of beds and borders. Most species are more airy, with a dainty refinement that I feel prompts one to place them well away from buildings. The modern and the old florist's roses are more suitable for use in conjunction with formality, whether it be of a wall, path or hedge. When the wall can be of grey Cotswold stone, or the hedge of a blend of holly and box and copper beech, the contrast is superb. A visit to Hidcote [Gloucestershire] will convince intending hedge-planters of a tapestry background that can be obtained from mixed hedges. For informal hedges the roses themselves present several varieties and species of great value.

It cannot be denied that a garden full of one thing can be boring to all but the ardent collector himself. While we are all entitled to do what we like with our gardens I would suggest a careful disposal of old roses, so that the eye may not tire of their qualities in perspective. The old roses create a delightful pattern of flower and foliage at six yards' distance, but at a greater distance give a rather spotty effect. This is due to their small leaves and the regular dotting of flowers along the branches.

I feel they very much need the foil of other foliage and the contrast of other flower shapes and styles. Particularly successful with these old roses are foxgloves – just the common wild type and the white with a few of 'Sutton's Primrose' placed near the dark purple forms. Their spikes give the right contrast in form, and their colours blend happily. Also I like to use *Lilium candidum* and some of the daintier delphiniums in light colours, and the tall irises of the *ochroleuca* section. The striking contrast of leaf and flower in these gives just the relief and 'uplift' that are needed. Foliage of the *Iris pallida* and *Sisyrinchium striatum*; *Eryngium giganteum*, the silvery grey biennial 'Sea Holly'; sages, the ordinary culinary and grey leaved form; Hosta or plantain lily of which the best is *Hosta sieboldiana*; *Stachys olympica*, and *Santolina neapolitana* and *chamaecyparissus* – all are splendid subjects for underplanting and mixing with the old roses. The blatant yellow blooms of the Santolina or 'Cotton Lavender' need never interfere with the colour scheme if the plants are clipped over in February. For bold cornerwork, especially against paved paths, the *Megesea Saxifrages* (*Bergenia*) provide the very best of materials, their big broad leathery leaves of dark green matching the stones' solidity.

These foliage plants can blend an otherwise jumbled mass of flowers and leaves into an harmonious and satisfying whole. The use of white flowers with the roses cannot be too strongly emphasised. For this purpose, I have already mentioned foxgloves and *Iris ochroleuca*, and to them will add Philadelphus or Mock Orange. A great range of these is available from small shrubs of 2–3 feet to giants up to 15 feet, and the blend of their fragrance with that of the roses can be almost overwhelming on a still summer evening. A quantity of pinks – a seed-raised garden strain is the best, embracing all the tones that are found in the 'Highland Hybrids' – 'White Ladies' and others will provide the most ideal display at just the right time, and their fragrance again enters into the scheme. White flowers will intensify the purples and enrich the pink roses; pale lilac, as may be obtained from *Campanula lactiflora*, will purify pink roses. Various contrasts, such as the clouds of greenish yellow stars and velvet leaves of *Alchemilla mollis* with 'Tuscany', will be found, and over them all a solid garden quality should reign. Flimsy annuals and ordinary daisy-flowers, so often the body of the average herbaceous border, may well be avoided.

It will be apparent from the above that I like my old roses mixed with other plants, rather than arrayed in beds by themselves. They can be very pleasingly grown in this way, but the general blend of flower and foliage which is apparent in a mixed border is to my mind more satisfying and appealing. In addition to creating a glorious picture at midsummer, many of the foliage plants will produce flowers earlier or later; a suitable grouping of spring bulbs, followed in late summer by Galtonias (summer hyacinths), the hardy *Agapanthus campanulatus* (*mooreanus*) and hybrids, and the free-flowering dwarf *Yucca flaccida* and *Y. filamentosa* will provide interest throughout the year. Over my more stalwart roses I have just planted some of the small hardy *Clematis viticella* varieties. These can be cut to the ground every February and will provide a canopy of glorious maroons, mauves, and whites to blend with fuchsias and agapanthus in late July and August. With the old roses, therefore, may I suggest a generous blend of flowers and foliage, to create a 'cottage garden' mixture, to give colour and interest from April to October.

Graham Stuart Thomas
The Old Shrub Roses
J.M. DENT
1957

Harvesting Herbs

Herb gardens are common today, but when HERB GARDENING, *the book from which this
is an extract, was written, few people had them. I know, because I desperately wanted one and
couldn't find the plants or the know-how.* CLAIRE LOEWENFELD *(died 1974), the founder
of the Chiltern Herb Farm, was an early pioneer, and her book discusses the cultivation,
uses and characters of most culinary herbs, as well as suggesting the occasional recipe.
Although first published more than forty years ago, it is still the herb-grower's bible.*

From February almost to November there are usually some herbs which can be
picked freshly, according to which herbs are grown – and during the months
from June to October fresh leaves and sprigs are available from most herbs and
the best possible use should be made of them.

There is, however, a peak time in the life of each herb during which it should be
cut for preserving – either by drying, the age-old natural way of preserving herbs – or
by the new way of freezing with which we have no long experience yet. Drying has
been infinitely improved lately by new knowledge and methods of how to retain the
important constituents; and the result is the 'green dried' herb, preserved by a process
which avoids loss of volatile oils and other active subtances, thus retaining the aroma,
colour and scent.

In order to achieve such results, the herbs have to be picked at the right moment,
when their volatile oil content is at its highest; this, with leafy herbs, is usually before they
go into flower. It lasts, in fact, from the time when flower buds begin to form until
they are half-open, though there are exceptions, such as parsley and chives, which can be
cut at any time, and sage and russian tarragon (for instance) which can develop strong
and unpleasant flavours unless harvested at an earlier moment. The oil content during the
day is at its highest before the sun becomes too hot, after the dew has dried, and therefore
it is best to cut the herbs in the morning as soon as the dew has dried on the foliage.

The effect of the active substances will diminish greatly if the plants or part of the
plants are collected immediately after dew or rain, and are still wet.

The content of volatile oil with certain leafy herbs increases up to the flowering
period, but then diminishes again.

Annual herbs may be cut within about four inches of the ground but perennial herbs should not be cut back more than about one-third. Most of the leafy herbs can be cut two or three times during the summer, depending on the weather. The perennial herbs should really not be cut after the end of September because the new growth will not harden before the cold weather comes. The plants should be cut possibly with a stainless-steel knife or in some cases with a hook, and should be collected in a flat-bottomed basket, garden truck or box, but never in a sack or bag. Crushing and bruising can happen so easily and a heap of herbs can heat up so quickly that it is important that all this should be avoided.

After the herbs have been cut they must be sorted out, and weeds and grass that may be mixed with them removed beforehand. Those leaves which are really encrusted with mud should also be discarded but loose dirt may be gently washed off with clear cool, but not cold, water. They should be shaken to get rid of excess moisture or the moisture should drip off the trays on which they should be put in a flat layer.

It is important that they should not be handled and stay too long in the water because some of the important nutrients and minerals may dissolve into the water. It is therefore also important to take the chill off the water, as the shock of cold water may diminish the content of nutrients.

Any deterioration before drying makes the dried herb useless and therefore they should never be collected unless they can be washed if necessary, spread out and dried immediately afterwards. No more should be collected at any one time than the capacity of the available drying space will take.

When flowers are used, they can only be harvested when they are fully open, and have to be collected whenever they open. Flowers are not washed at all but are handled very carefully, not pressed, not heaped. They should not be overripe, wilting or discolouring as then the volatile oil may already be diminished. Whole and unblemished flowers are necessary for drying or crystallising or using for any other purpose. Seed herbs, such as dill and fennel, have the seeds gathered when the heads turn brown; the heads can be tested for cutting by tapping the stems each day after they begin to turn brown – if the seeds fall when tapped they are ready to cut. The umbels should be removed with the little stem attached and the heads can be collected in a box to prevent seeds from falling to the ground, or hung upside down to dry and the seeds should drop on to paper or into muslin bags tied over the flower heads to catch the seeds.

The difficulty in collecting seeds at the right moment lies in the fact that when they are really mature they drop down and are lost.

Berries are collected when the fruit is ripe and the colour at its richest, before they become soft or darken. Too much handling is a great disadvantage and should be avoided under all circumstances.

The roots are harvested in late autumn when the leaves have already started to discolour. They have to be well washed and brushed before drying.

Much depends on the time of the day, the right time in the cycle of the plant, the speed with which the herbs can be collected, washed, freed from the excess moisture and dried. From the moment they are collected they should be prevented from being exposed to sun or light and they should be in the drying places at the earliest possible moment.

Claire Loewenfeld
Herb Gardening
FABER AND FABER
1964

Town Gardens

*It's not surprising that this admirable advice on coping with the dreariest town garden
is given with military precision. Before becoming a garden designer, the author,*
KENNETH MIDGLEY, *drove a tank in a Special Service Squadron.
After that, he became an instructor in camouflage – something rather
useful when tackling a town garden with all the normal faults.*

The little town garden, one of those tiny squares or narrow strips of land lying behind a tall terrace house in the heart of a town or city, presents difficulties, many of which are unconnected with its lack of size. It might even be said that, to some people, its restricted area is an advantage in that it saves work in much the same way as does a small house. This is true since any effort is concentrated and can be just so much more meticulous, and any materials or plants required can never be in a great quantity, so that there is an obvious saving in expense. Furthermore, it is possible to produce a peaceful retreat within its narrow confines as in any acre, given the right conditions.

What do we find? If we assume for a moment that the house is old there will be remnants of an earlier garden, possibly a tree or a number of young sycamore saplings, a thicket of old privet, a laurel or aucuba, and laurustinus, and an odd accumulation of old stone and brick. The plot may be shut in by tall buildings which not only make it look smaller than it really is, but cast dense shadows. These buildings may have windows at a high level robbing the site of privacy.

The soil is probably stale, impoverished, and structureless, either brick-like clay or fine dust, and the air is polluted with smoke, dust and industrial fumes. There may even be only one way in — through the house, although a number of strange cats will find entry no difficulty at all. Not a promising start, but fortunately these obstacles are not always found together. Some can be altered and others mitigated, and the garden must be planned to suit those which have to remain.

These town plots can vary enormously in size, shape, aspect and surroundings and each will call for careful and individual attention. My suggestion is that you deal first with the fundamental questions and decide the purpose of the garden. You alone know the answer to this. Follow this by going through your own requirements. Is the garden something to be looked at from the house, a place into which you go only for its maintenance? In this case you will be creating a 'picture' or something rather like a stage set where the audience is not allowed behind the scenes. This can be intriguing and if you visualize your garden as a stage you will find yourself creating interest and a sense of depth with commanding plants at the sides of your setting rather like stage wings. You may even cheat by using smaller-growing plants in the distance than those in the foreground, dark colours beyond light, or by making lines which the eye expects to be parallel converge slightly (e.g. sides of a path).

If your viewpoint from the house is a high oblique, as from an upper window, you will be conscious of the ground pattern and in winter particularly you will want to look down on pleasing shapes in a nicely balanced arrangement. In either case space required for movement will be confined to servicing and greater areas can be devoted to plants.

Perhaps you will have time to sit in the garden and, unlike the suburban and country plots where there is some latitude, your choice of an area for this will be restricted and the chosen point may well become the nucleus for your design. It is no use devoting an area to chairs and table if it is in perpetual shade or is in full morning sun whereas your only free time is in the evening, if it is overlooked by neighbours' windows, or in such a position that conversation, except in whispers, is impossible. You will never use it. Consider also the question of access. If you are entertaining you will want to avoid a precarious walk with a tray; a site near the house might be better, particularly as it is within earshot of the telephone.

If your house is beautiful what nicer than to sit facing it? On the other hand, through no fault of yours it may be quite ugly and then you are better with your back to it. These considerations – and you will be able to think of others – are often in conflict, and one must strike a happy medium.

A matter for early decision is that of the level of the garden, since some variation adds interest if it can be contrived. A way of doing this which immediately comes to mind is to sink part of it, but the temptation should be resisted until thought has been given to the dispersal of surface water which will inevitably collect in the lower ground. The presence of a fairly deep water drain which can be entered will satisfy the conditions, so will the making of a soakaway (a deep hole packed with hardcore or stone) in light or gravelly land, but on clay digging a sunken garden is inviting trouble.

When the garden is separated from the building by an 'area' there is freedom in the establishment of the garden level, but where it abuts on to the house, the level must be clear of the air bricks or, as in all other cases, 6 in. below the damp-proof course. A slight fall over the garden site of even 1 ft can be utilized to create a shallow terrace, a change in level retained by a dwarf wall or raised bed.

Kenneth Midgley
Garden Design
PENGUIN
1966

two-year-old wood but if possible last season's shoots of such slow-growing hard-wooded plants as maples, witch hazel and magnolias.

The only equipment needed is a spade, some pieces of wire bent in hairpin fashion, a batch of two-foot canes and a barrowload of a mixture of sand, peat and soil. I take out half a spadeful of soil just where the branch will meet the soil and replace it with the compost. Then I scratch the bark with the thumb nail at this point, or twist it if it is tough, and peg it down with wire into the soil.

Beside each layer a cane is used to hold the branch upright, partly because it produces a balanced plant, but also because it helps divert the sap flow to the wounded, pegged-down point, from which roots will be produced.

While the general run of shrubs, including shrub roses, propagated in this trouble-free manner, do produce new plants by the following autumn, layers from the hard-wooded types and rhododendrons are rarely safe to move for another year.

So popular is the blessed thing, the loganberry without thorns, that I can never raise enough to pass on. But like all its kind, the blackberries and hybrids from them, it can be increased from so-called tip layers.

This means that you do not need to use a whole branch. You simply peg down the tips of the branches and each will become a new plant in six to eight weeks. Not only can you get a new plant from each of the old branches, while arching it in a fashion that will make picking easier, but you can even use the new season's growths when they are sufficiently well developed.

The same technique can be adopted for increasing rambler roses, and some climbers respond, though not all, I have found. The clematis a friend admired can also be propagated successfully by layering, though in this case into a pot of sandy soil set in the ground.

Rooting cuttings of many kinds of plants on an everyday home scale has become much less a hit-or-miss process with the use of polythene covering instead of glass. You simply put the cuttings in a pot of moist light soil, insert three or four stakes, then draw a polythene bag over the lot and secure with an elastic band round the pot, and then stand it in a light position; there is little more to it than that.

The broad principle behind this elemental piece of horticultural practice is that you must keep the leaves charged with moisture until roots have formed and begin to replace the natural loss. To this end, cuttings standing in closed glass frames are sprayed over several times a day. Under polythene, provided air is not admitted, spraying is unnecessary. The cuttings remain turgid in the close atmosphere induced.

Cuttings of shrubs of most kinds can be rooted in this very simple way, some roses too; all are worth trying. It is certainly important annually to strike cuttings of shrubs that have a limited span anyway, like cistus and ceanothus, or which eventually grow too ungainly to be allowed to live out their natural days in the garden and are better replaced by their younger scions.

The shoots used for cuttings must be of the current season's growth; neither soft nor ripened yet into a hard condition. They are preferably pulled off this parent growth to come away with what gardeners call a 'heel', which must be trimmed of its tag of loose bark. Otherwise if this would make them too long, they are actually cut off, making the cut with a razor blade just below a leaf joint; the lower leaves are stripped off and sometimes the tip, if the cutting is inclined to be whippy. Dipping the ends in hormone powder sold for the purpose makes rooting more certain.

The soil mixture to use must be open, as gardeners call it, three parts of sharp sand being mixed with one of loam and two of peat. But fertiliser-treated rooting media – hardly more expensive and cleaner to use – are now on sale. If these are used in small fibre pots impregnated with fertiliser, producing new plants from cuttings becomes a quick and sure process involving the least possible trouble.

Fred Whitsey
Sunday Telegraph Gardening Book
COLLINS
1966

Particular Peonies

This book by GEOFFREY SMITH (1928–2009), once the superintendent of the
Harlow Carr gardens in Yorkshire, was one of the books I bought when trying to create
my first garden, a mere 15 miles from Harrogate, where Smith's book originated.
I would still recommend it to beginners – far better than
'Difficult Plants for Easy Places'.

The history of the genus *Paeonia* alone would fill a book, should anyone find the time to accumulate the wealth of legend and romance which has been woven around it. Pliny even goes as far as to call it the oldest of all plants, but on what authority I do not know. In my garden there is a young plant taken as a layer from a patriarchal specimen in a garden near Pickering, known to be at least 108 years old. The plant is said to be possessed of great healing properties, and indeed, takes its name from Paeon, first physician to the gods.

Paeonia lactiflora, introduced in 1784 by a Russian and then in 1805 by Banks, has given rise, so the authorities on the subject write, to many beautiful garden forms introduced from China from the early part of the 19th century. Since then, of course, the European hybridists have worked hard to improve on the original varieties available, with considerable success. A glance through any specialist's catalogue will show what a great number there are to choose from, and it would be impossible to list them here. 'Sarah Bernhardt', clear pink; 'Kelway's Glorious', white and fragrant; 'Bowl of Beauty', cherry red with a cream central boss of stamens; and 'Karl Rosenfield', wine red, are all excellent.

Seed is the easy way to increase stocks of the species, but it should be taken only from parents selected for the quality of their flowers. Named forms are increased by division.

Of all this beautiful genus, *Paeonia mlokosewitschii* is my particular favourite. Not only is it the first to flower in this garden, but from the glaucous-green leaves to the primrose-yellow flowers, 5–6 in. across, it is a breathtaking sight when in full bloom. Compared to the species already described this is a dwarf, only 15–18 in. high. The flowers appear in May, rather later than in other more sheltered gardens. Propagation, as with other species, is by seed. A word of warning when sowing seed of any peony, make certain the mice cannot gain access to them or nothing will be left but empty husks.

Paeonia veitchii woodwardii is an even dwarfer plant than *P. mlokosewitschii*. The habit is so neat, the leaves so finely and deeply cut, that I like to grow my plants amongst the dwarf shrubs on the outskirts of the rock garden. The ultimate height is only a modest 12 in., and the flowers are a fine, soft rose-pink. There are certain plants which once seen can never be forgotten, and this has certainly been the case with the white-flowered form of *woodwardii* which I saw for the first and last time in a famous Northumberland garden. Should any reader have the good fortune to be offered a dainty, white-flowered peony with a central boss of scarlet stamens, do not enquire into its parentage. Take the parcel carefully, and with suitable reverence plant it in the place of honour, then ever afterwards pay homage to the shrine.

Seed offers a means of increase, but whether the bees were to blame or not, some of my seedlings had flowers of a rather unpleasant magenta. Fortunately those which lost caste in such a light-hearted manner can always be given to less popular garden visitors.

Geoffrey Smith
Easy Plants for Difficult Places
DAVID & CHARLES
1967

Determined Plants

COLLINGWOOD INGRAM (1880–1981) *spent fifty years plant-hunting throughout the world before writing his book* A GARDEN OF MEMORIES, *from which this extract is taken. In that time he learned much about the behaviour of plants – some of it inexplicable, as he describes – and how best to site them in the garden.*

I have never yet succeeded in making a species reverse the rhythm of its growing and resting periods. If an antipodean plant has become accustomed to grow throughout a southern hemisphere summer – namely from about October to February – being introduced into a northern hemisphere country it will not attempt to grow during those same calendar months but will insist on doing so during the summer months of its new home, say from March to August. Similarly if a plant has acquired the habit of becoming vegetatively active as soon as an autumnal rainy season starts – this is the usual procedure with most Cape Province species – on reaching England it will always begin growing, rain or no rain, at the beginning of our autumn and not as is usual with most plants, in our spring.

This determination of a plant to stick to the seasons it has been used to was once demonstrated to me in a very emphatic manner. In 1938 I was bringing home by sea a number of seedling trees and shrubs I had collected in Chile. These had all been gathered in the southern part of that country during the latter half of February – a month equivalent to our August. When they were uprooted their active season was, therefore, coming to an end and their sap in consequence would be starting to descend. Normally, I suppose, they would not have become vegetatively active again until the following September or October (months corresponding to our March and April). Yet, no sooner did the ship I was travelling in enter the temperate latitudes of the northern hemisphere – which she did early in April than, mirabile dictu! – the majority of my Chilean seedlings started to make new young growth. By what means were those antipodean plants able to discriminate between a vernal and an autumnal equinox? I doubt if that question will ever be answered. It was certainly not by a difference in temperature or by the amount of moisture they were receiving; nor could light hours have had anything to do with it, for during both equinoxes a day's length is of course identical in both hemispheres. Indeed it would seem to be a phenomenon that will admit of no logical explanation.

Incredible though it may seem I once lost, not from cold but from warmth, a lot of plants that were natives of a locality only a degree or two from the Equator. These were all seemingly killed by the heat they were subjected to in only a moderately hot English summer! I had raised the plants – a very mixed lot – from some seed that had been gathered by an engineer friend in a locality only just below the perpetual snowline in the Venezuelan Andes. Coming as they did from a great height and near the Equator, they were no doubt used to an all-the-year-round, uniformly cool climate. They could not, therefore, stand even the moderate warmth of one of our English summers.

I have always maintained that the correct siting of a plant is one of, if not the most important factor leading to its successful culture. Knowledge of a plant's natural habitat, and having some idea of the ecological conditions it is living in, are of course valuable clues in the choice of its site. Unfortunately in a garden like mine, which has been established for a number of years, it is often difficult, if not impossible, to benefit by such knowledge: the position you think would be most likely to suit your new plant's requirement will almost certainly be already occupied by some other subject.

Collingwood Ingram
A Garden of Memories
WITHERBY
1970

Glorious Scents

The book by CHRISTOPHER LLOYD (1921–2006) *from which this extract
is taken was my inspiration when I first began gardening, and I have loved it ever since.
It was difficult to pick out a single piece from it, but, perhaps because I am writing
this in August with a huge bunch of old-fashioned sweet peas on the table,
the following passage seems appropriate.*

The weather in August is often docile without being fiercely hot. On some days the sun breaks quickly through a dense early-morning mist. At the same time our mulberries give a sleepy heave, as a first breath of wind stirs them, and the only violent branch movements in the garden are caused by bouncing sparrows. On other days it is moistly cloudy but still quiet – a kind of weather gardeners can enjoy, since the light is gentle and flowers look well beneath it. Either way, the garden exhales an abundance of delicious scents.

The annual carnations are good wafters, once they get going. All the colours, even the whites (which are so drearily odourless in the florists' soulless brand) contribute generously. I always have odd plants of mignonette scattered about the garden at strategic points and sometimes grow a few in pots, which I can move around. 'Does mignonette ever smell like it used to?' I was asked rather querulously by one elderly visitor as though the Bomb, the cost of living and Labour government must between them have put an end to all such pleasures. Well, it does; but you never quite know when. Sometimes its spicy fragrance reaches you most powerfully by night; at others, when the sun is on the flowers. All you can do is to wait for it, because nothing comes of sticking your face into the plant. Always grow the commonest sort of 'unimproved' mignonette. Those of more robust and upright habit or bolder colouring are less fragrant.

Petunias smell strongest in the evening, like their relatives, the nicotianas, but the bedding verbenas belong to daytime. All except the pure scarlet strains are well scented. Stocks, too, are daytimers; the night-scented brand has quite a different quality, with something of almond essence in it. Most varieties of the modern sweet pea need to be gathered together in large numbers before they yield appreciable fragrance. I was much struck, a few years ago, by a hedge of purple sweet peas growing in the Northern Horticultural Society's gardens at Harlow Carr, by Harrogate [Yorkshire]. Their flowers were small and without the large, wavy standard petal and open wings of the modern strains, but the scent was of a voluptuous richness such as one had forgotten a sweet pea could possess. This was the old-fashioned *Grandiflora* type of 60 years ago, before the modern Spencer varieties had monopolised the market.

Of the shrubs, *Hoheria sexstylosa* is radiant throughout August, with pearl-like buds and white star flowers among gleaming foliage, piled up in billows to a height of 15 ft. It has the characteristic honey scent of other hoherias, and the flowers make a particularly flattering background for the newly emerged brood of red admiral and peacock butterflies, with which it is popular.

Anyone with an acid soil can grow the sweet-pepper bush, *Clethra alnifolia*, which carries spikes of warmly fragrant, small white flowers in late summer. The bush likes moisture. It then grows 8 ft tall and gradually spreads by suckering.

Better than the scent of the few roses that are flowering at this between-seasons period is the stewed-apple fragrance of the sweet-briar. I have a seedling near a garden seat and I prune it hard every year so that it is stimulated into strong growth from spring to autumn.

Lonicera japonica 'Halliana' is much more inclined to waft by day as well as by night than are most honeysuckles, such as the Late Dutch. The hair-oil fragrance of *Clematis heracleifolia davidiana* is powerful on some days. Spartium is always good; the hebes that are related to *H. salicifolia* – 'Miss E. Fittall', 'Hidcote' and 'Midsummer Beauty' – are very sweet. Spiciest fragrance of all is given off by the common myrtle *Myrtus communis*, in its August–September hey-day. It is like an etherealised version of the goodly smell of crushed myrtle leaves.

The smell of hydrangeas is seldom mentioned. It is neither pleasant nor unpleasant; a sort of vegetable aroma, slightly acrid and quite insistent at times. I enjoy it. Phloxes, which look so well with hydrangeas, are the most bountiful of the herbaceous plants for scent at this time.

I have always been puzzled by a globe thistle that I originally acquired from a friend's garden solely on account of its scent being strongly reminiscent of carnations. This is *Echinops sphaerocephalus*, a six-footer with ugly foliage and undistinguished grey flower heads. It has never given off the same scent since I have had it. But it is not unusual for flowers to smell differently at different times and in different places just as vegetables can vary in their flavours.

Christopher Lloyd
The Well-Tempered Garden
COLLINS
1970

Ferns for the Garden

JOHN RAVEN (1914–1980) and his wife, Faith (parents, by the way,
of writer Sarah Raven), were lucky enough to have two gardens in Britain that
could not be more different. Ardtornish, on the west coast of Scotland, has high rainfall
and acid soil and is near the warm Gulf Stream. Shepreth in East Anglia is slightly
alkaline, has one of the lowest rainfalls in the country and endures heavy frosts.
But in both, the writer has managed to cultivate British ferns.

The fernery, beloved of the Victorians, is almost as much a thing of the past as the Victorian bustle. Few except botanical gardens now boast a systematic collection of ferns set aside in a special bed, or sometimes even a separate corner of the garden. True, many gardens in Britain, especially in the north and west, contain several species of native ferns, put there usually by nature, both on old walls and in shady or boggy corners, and the addition is usually a welcome one. And true again, there is in many a narrow border, as dry as dust, which is inhospitable to almost everything except ferns but in which many of them thrive happily. The garden at Ardtornish falls emphatically into the former category; without even going out to count them I can think of at least ten native species which grow there unprompted and unaided by man. The garden at Shepreth, on the other hand, falls equally emphatically into the other category and contains by nature, even on the old walls with which it is so plentifully endowed, not a single species of fern. But it does possess, at the foot of an old barn and measuring some thirty feet in length by three in breadth, exactly such a border as I have just described. Here, over the past sixteen years since we bought the house, we have introduced about twenty species of fern, and have intermingled them, in what many visitors of the garden notice as an unusually attractive harmony, with the tall and beautiful, albeit very common British sedge, *Carex pendula*, which sows itself freely in the gravel path beside, but which can be controlled with the utmost ease and is anyhow surprisingly often accepted by other gardeners as a welcome present. Other accidental introductions which have come into the same border with the roots of the commoner British ferns include meadowsweet, which flourishes beside a leaky old barrel put there to catch the rainfall from the barn roof, wood-sorrel and sanicle, which came in with the beech fern or the oak fern that we brought down from Ardtornish, and, from the same source but less happily, because it spreads fast and far by fragile white underground stolons, enchanter's nightshade. Some of the ferns, notably the beech and the oak, *Adiantum pedatum*, and a very rare one that we found in local abundance in the hills behind Cannes, *Asplenium jahandiezii*, have not unreasonably so much resented the change of environment that they have with varying rapidity died on us. But sufficient of the rest remain and spread to stock other unpromising patches, not only of our garden, but of other people's as well.

Nevertheless the impression must not be given that all ferns, even when they are native to the British Isles, can be trusted to look after themselves. Not so long ago we suffered under that delusion at Shepreth and, as I have already recited, we paid quite dearly for it. The smaller ferns in particular, being in the main accustomed to plenty of bare space and fresh air, so resent the overcrowding of a fern border that they are best planted, if not in a wall or on a natural outcrop of rock, then in a crevice in the rockery or in a sink. Even the fern border itself, for all but the commonest and most accommodating species, imposes a few simple demands: ideally it requires not only protection from the fiercest wind and heat but also sharp drainage and a decent modicum of humus in the soil. And even when all this is provided, there will still remain some species, whether calcicolous or calcifuge, that are not easily satisfied. Like the majority of other plants, most ferns have their own particular fads and fancies; and who are we to blame them on that account?

John Raven
A Botanist's Garden
COLLINS
1971

What Makes a Plant Garden-Worthy?

When I asked an expert gardener and writer which book he would recommend
for the tyro gardener or for those who felt they were lamentably ignorant, HUGH JOHNSON's
(born 1939) THE PRINCIPLES OF GARDENING, *from which this passage is taken,*
was his immediate choice. What I particularly like about the book — apart from its depth of
knowledge — is the prose style. It's clear, concise, doesn't patronize and is full of opinions
(as befits a former SUNDAY TIMES *journalist). See for yourself.*

There is an old Hollywood comic's gag: 'New is easy. Funny is hard.' There has never (or not for four hundred years), been a shortage of new plants to grow in gardens. But whether they have been better than the old ones is not always clear. It depends on what the gardener is looking for. There are so many aspects of quality in plants that it is worth pausing to consider what makes a good candidate for our limited space.

There is a rough and ready division, of course, between the beautiful and the useful. Any plant that can fairly claim to be both has a head start. But there are many other categories of plant character that have their garden uses. Critical gardeners keep a mental score card of points for and against plants in order to decide whether they are suffered to remain, enthusiastically propagated, or are torn up and consigned to the bonfire.

Most fundamental — except perhaps to a masochist kind of gardener most often found in an alpine house — is a good constitution; a plant's ability to thrive and wax fat. This does not mean the hooligan temperament of a weed, but the inclination, given an appropriate site, to grow steadily and strongly without sudden fits of the vapours. If shoots regularly die back, or a succession of pests and diseases make it their headquarters, or the plant sits in an apparent coma, it may of course be the gardener's fault. But once he has satisfied himself that he has given it a fair chance it must either thrive or be scrapped. I can think of otherwise unexceptional plants whose chief beauty lies in their rubicund appearance of enjoying life. It is a principal virtue of the tulips (and many other bulbs); the peony; some wild roses; planes; willows; many pines.

A more specialised form of the same virtue is to be able to thrive where little else can. Plants thus acquire local merit points which do not apply elsewhere. Few trees will stand a full salt-laden sea blast, for example. The sycamore, often regarded as little better than a weed, has won its battle honours as first line of defence against salty south-westerlies – a lop-sided thing, perhaps, but tough enough to allow something better to grow in its lee.

Similarly there are plants adapted to what can scarcely be called soil; grasses that can bind shifting sand, heathers for dark peat, gorse for dry heathland or spindle for chalk.

In Arctic winters the ability to survive at all makes a plant garden-worthy, whereas in temperate places the sheer perversity of gardeners gives an extra half-point for glamour to plants that are liable to succumb when the occasional hard winter arrives.

Straightforward speed of growth is one of the most obvious qualities a gardener may be looking for. Hedge-plants are generally (but mistakenly) judged on how soon they will reach the required height. The word 'vigour' means both speed and overall willingness to keep growing. But very slow growth is a character equally in demand. Small gardens need scaled-down plants. There is a premium on tiny shrubs and dwarf conifers that take a long time to reach saleable size.

If flowers are the first thing to come to mind as desirable in a garden, there are many ways of judging the quality of a flower. There are those who see true beauty only in naturally evolved balance and proportion of wild flowers, whether from Sikkim or a local ditch. Others judge a flower on the breeder's success in packing the maximum number of petals. Others count on the brilliance of its colour. Others put stress on its oddness. A blue rose would be a best-seller regardless of its intrinsic merit. Very few have the depth of knowledge to judge the merits of a flower in the context of its peers, its ancestors, its breeding history and its record in cultivation.

The shape, colour, texture, scent, leaves and habit of a flower are all matters for critical debate. But there are other aspects beside its looks. A plant may gain merit by flowering earlier or later than others and so extending the season for that genus or species – or the very same quality may tell against it by making it liable to damage by late or early frosts.

The length of its flowering season is critical too. Most of the saga of rose-breeding over the last 180 years has been concerned with making the term 'perpetual' come true. Such autumn flowers as Michaelmas daisies and chrysanthemums have immensely long periods in bloom. If the poppy flowered at that time of year it could not compete.

Flowers which having flowered die well or leave beautiful seed heads are worth extra points: those that leave sorry brown rags lose merit. There is extra credit, too, for flowers that dry off the stem still keeping their perfect form, or that can be picked and dried. Dried delphiniums keep their potent blue.

Scent is a quality not much discussed except in general terms and little understood. There is a small category of plants grown as much for their scent as for their other qualities. Such herbs as lavender, rosemary and mint; summer jasmine and Dutch honeysuckle; philadelphus; balsam poplar are examples. With most plants, though – even with roses which surely have a duty to be fragrant – we put too little stress on scent.

Flavour was once the chief criterion for fruit and vegetables. Now it is considered secondary to appearance, uniformity and regularity of cropping. The reason for this is because expensive research takes commercial factors into account first. But this is a powerful argument for the planting and study of old sorts by amateurs who want taste, not supermarket shelf-life.

This is only to touch on the inexhaustible list of contributions that plants can make to gardens. Thorny plants make good barriers. Some plants take kindly to clipping and grow dense and snug. Some make dramatic gestures and some take up quaint poses. Some cover the ground as close as a rug and save us having to weed. Some we love for their anthology of associations. Some we must have simply because they are rare.

Hugh Johnson
The Principles of Gardening
MITCHELL BEAZLEY
1979

The Weekend Garden

All of us lucky enough to own weekend retreats puzzle how to keep the garden looking respectable without spending every day there. ANNE SCOTT-JAMES (*born* 1913), *former editor of* HARPER'S BAZAAR *magazine, and the wife of cartoonist Osbert Lancaster, writes here from experience. I would go along exactly with her advice, perhaps adding that wild plants that flourish in the countryside around you are another good source.*

Extra Help: The weekend garden must not become a tyranny, and if there is any chance of getting a few hours' help in the course of the week, the weekender will seize it; I am lucky to have a pensioner one day a week. The priority jobs to be done in my absence are mowing and watering and my parting words are always 'Whatever happens, Percy, mow the grass.' Nothing gives a better finish to a garden than mown grass, and nothing is more depressing than to leave a tidy garden on a Sunday night and arrive the following weekend to find the lawn shaggy and spotted with dandelions. Selective watering is also essential, or one will lose plants in dry weather. Young plants, transplanted plants and plants in pots will need a drink between Sunday and Friday. If I had nobody to water, I would cut out pots altogether.

A Simple Structure: Here I speak from failure, not in the proud accents of success, for my garden is not labour-saving, and if I didn't have Percy I would simplify the design of the garden whatever the outlay. I would have brick paths instead of grass paths, would build a wall to enclose the front garden, replacing the old mixed country hedge which takes so much clipping, and lay paving instead of grass wherever possible; in short, I would replace the most labour-intensive plants (grass and hedges) with hardware. The cottage gardens of the Cotswolds and the Lake District always look beautifully neat inside their dry-stone walls, which can be embroidered with rock plants. If I ever make this change, I shall use the best possible materials – good bricks or cobbles and real stone, for texture is important to me. If I could find an old-fashioned craftsman, I would like my paths laid in a herring-bone or other traditional pattern, perhaps with sections of cobbles let into an attractive pattern of bricks. These changes would be extremely expensive, so I muddle on, but a simpler design would not only save labour, it would be more attractive to the eye. Strong, simple outlines make the best background to mixed planting.

Good Weekend Plants: Trees and shrubs are an obvious choice, and many weekend gardeners confine themselves to these alone. When our elms were felled I planted some hardwood trees as a matter of conscience, including a Turkey Oak (*Quercus cerris*) and a weeping beech. I still water them in summer, but in a year or two they should be safely established. My other trees – a walnut, a chestnut, some field maples, an ash, a group of the lovely silvery-leaved *Sorbus aria lutescens*, a willow-leaved pear, and a few conifers – take care of themselves entirely.

Shrubs, of course, I have in multitudes and they give me no trouble at all. All they ask is an annual pruning after flowering, or a clipping-over in spring, and as pruning is the garden job I enjoy most I find my shrubs totally undemanding. I have a succession of flowering shrubs from the scented, pink-budded *Viburnum carlesii* of March to the winter mahonias, with *Spiraea arguta*, lilacs, deutzias, shrub roses, *Kolkwitzia amabilis*, various philadelphus, *Hypericum patulum* 'Hidcote' and many others in between.

But if most shrubs can fend for themselves, many smaller plants cannot long survive without human help except in heavy ground or a district with high rainfall. A weekend garden is likely to be a thirsty garden, with the hoe and the hose out of action for five days a week.

The best way of conserving moisture in the soil is certainly to mulch, and I try to blanket the sunnier beds in spring with compost and the rosebeds with farm manure. But mulches have a way of disappearing and in a dry summer shallow-rooted plants will suffer without water. I have regretfully given up such plants as phlox, bergamot and astilbes and concentrate on deep-rooting plants like achilleas, tansy, *Salvia superba*, Japanese anemones, acanthus, alchemillas, peonies and astrantias.

To mix with the deep-rooting herbaceous plants I use many rock plants and plants of the Mediterranean which will thrive in full sun: helianthemums, aubrietias, sedums, cottage pinks, cistuses, *Phlomis fruticosa*, and many euphorbias. My favourite cistus, C. *purpureus*, with crinkly pink flowers blotched with purple has transformed a particularly dry bed in my garden, where a tall cypress robs the soil, into a well-filled corner.

velvet buds, with no leaves unfurled to detract from their exotic beauty. Visitors seeing the first flowers dropped on the green grass wonder where they have come from, looking in vain from left to right, not thinking to look at the great tree above their heads. Some years the branches sweep down to eye level and then we are all bewitched. Our tree loved the rich, deep soil and shot up like a rocket, all of 6 ft/ 2 m a year. But it has paid the price for such exuberance, for twice now several large, brittle limbs have been torn off by autumn gales; rough pruning! The large, soft, heart-shaped leaves, which do not expand fully till mid-June, make pretty dappled shade for the large bed underneath.

More trees planted for shade were *Liriodendron tulipifera*, *Catalpa bignonioides*, *Liquidambar styraciflua*, a pink-flowered Robinia (torn to pieces by wind), *Picea omorika* and *Gingko biloba*. What a list, far too many for the space available, and there were shrubs as well. The blue-berried *Symplocos paniculata* was ruined by the sticky spit from aphids in the oak above. A Neillia made a thicket of stems (useful for pheasant cover, in suitable places), pretty in leaf and flower, but menacing here.

I have found that though, in places, I have underground moisture I do have to restrict the number of trees that suck it up greedily in dry summers, leaving my plants between famished.

At the beginning some shade was already provided by the high canopy of alder and oak, so I planted great clumps of hostas backed by tall stands of Solomon's Seal, *Polygonatum* × *hybridum*, and the common fern, the Male Fern, *Dryopteris filix-mas*. Among them, for good ground cover, I planted *Tiarella cordifolia* and *Geranium endressii*, both of which spread quickly, making a carpet of pretty foliage as well as providing a foam of white or pink flowers in spring. Lily-of-the-Valley seemed the right thing to plant, bluebells were already there (why not keep them?) and the Welsh Poppy, *Meconopsis cambrica*, in orange and lemon, added to a spring picture of simple charm. But the bluebells and Lily-of-the-Valley spread far too well, pushing their way through clumps of Tellima and jostling poor Bowles' Golden Grass, *Milium effusum* 'Aureum', almost out of existence. The poppies too were into everything. After a few years my ruthless character could stand it no longer and all those invasive creatures had to come out and be banished to places where I felt they could do less damage.

The upper side of this bed was drier, partly because of tree roots, so I planted it with things that enjoyed the spring and early summer moisture. Pretty little *Corydalis solida* is very welcome there early in the spring, while Erythroniums have increased well. *Erythronium dens-canis* and *E. californicum* 'White Beauty' do especially well. They come up through carpets of *Viola riviniana* Purpurea Group (previously, but wrongly, known as

Viola labradorica) which I find invaluable for awkward conditions. Dwarf vincas and *Leptinella squalida* are the only things that have made a satisfactory carpet over the roots of *Acer davidii*. This is a most beautiful small tree, especially in winter when its green-and-white-striped bark is tinted red and all the young twigs are coral against a blue sky. I think it should be in grass. It makes such a loofah-like mat of roots.

On the lower damper side of this bed are hybrids of *Primula vulgaris*; P. 'Guinevere' and P. 'Lady Greer' look well mixed up in backgrounds of pink- and purple-leafed ajugas. Very striking too are a few clumps of P. 'Cowichan' Garnet Group. I love best the darkest garnet colours, velvet soft, with the merest glint of a golden eye. Various forms of *Anemone nemorosa*, including the fragile-looking lilac-blue bowls of *A. n.* 'Robinsoniana' run now with Tiarella, while *Potentilla rupestris* looks right with sprays of pure white flowers on rosy-pink stems. *Heucherella alba* 'Bridget Bloom' has settled happily and flowers over a long season in this bed, but the ordinary heucheras would not put roots down into the sour black silt.

Beth Chatto
The Damp Garden
DENT 1982; CASSELL ILLUSTRATED,
A DIVISION OF OCTOPUS PUBLISHING GROUP LTD
2005

I'm a Lime

*Everyone who insists that specimen trees need to be sited with accuracy probably
follows the method used by John Fowler (the English interior designer) — though perhaps
rather more dourly than as described here by* DEBORAH CAVENDISH, DUCHESS OF
DEVONSHIRE *(born 1920). When you position an important eye-catcher — probably
no more than a twig in its infancy — in the garden, you need to remember how
the full-sized version will look from every possible angle, including indoors.*

It is sad to see the decline in confidence of the architectural profession and their patrons in the twentieth century. Can you imagine one of the giants of the seventeenth or eighteenth century showing his client a plan with a lot of little trees dotted about to distract the eye from the nasty building he has drawn? It seems to be the practice now to add whitebeams and birches, … never a proper oak or beech. I wonder if it is all done in an office, or if they go outside like John Fowler did when he became as interested in gardens as he was in curtains: he used to leave his client in the drawing-room and go into the garden, stop and raise his arms above his head shouting, 'I'm a lime.' The client was supposed to know if he was in the right place and had the rare chance to assert his authority by moving him a foot or two to right or left. Then John would throw himself on the ground in an attitude of prayer murmuring, 'I'm a prostrate rosemary.' He never suggested birches or whitebeams.

Duchess of Devonshire
The House: A Portrait of Chatsworth
MACMILLAN
1982

Magnificent Magnolias

*History don, biographer of Alexander the Great, and gardening columnist
for the* FINANCIAL TIMES, ROBIN LANE FOX *(born 1946) comes close to
being a Renaissance man. His first book,* BETTER GARDENING, *combines wit,
information, advice and passion, here expended on his favourite shrub.*

Better shrubs begin, for my money, with the best of all, the Magnolia. There is no older shrub on the market, for Magnolias grew beside primitive moorlands some hundred million years ago. They are far superior to birds and bees. Beetles attend their cool scent and pollinate the flowers, groping blindly inside their white cups. In the days of the dinosaur, the world's other pollinators were not yet at large. The Magnolia, moreover, is much too venerable to bother with such recent inventions as petals. Having neither a petal nor a sepal, its flowers caused botanists to panic. In an erudite compromise, they ruled that they were made of tepals.

These tepals hang downwards or sideways, project upwards like stars or candles, come in all colours from pale pink to chocolate purple and breathe some memorable scents. Perhaps you can put a name to all their varieties already, but you may still wonder which is the best for your soil and surface area.

The Magnolias are at home in America and south-east Asia. It is unlikely that there are any good hardy varieties waiting to be found in unexplored areas of China and Japan. The tender varieties are less familiar, though they would loom large in any full family gathering. I have never seen a jungle Magnolia in a botanical garden's hothouse, and there may yet be surprises in the forms lost in West China. Meanwhile, we have hardy Magnolias in plenty, for the garden varieties are mostly resistant to our vilest winters. I have never seen Magnolias with thicker trunks than those *soulangeana* forms down the boulevards of Washington where the winters excel anything we would tolerate here. The Magnolia's enemy is not so much the frost, in most garden forms, as their owners' forking and busybodying. After a hundred million years, they resent interference. Those big trees which run wild in forgotten gardens have made the most of the peace round their brittle, fleshy roots. 'Magnolias', writes Neil Treseder, their British expert, 'will usually tolerate complete neglect.' That is most obliging.

When you want a Magnolia, therefore, you must plan the permanency and look far ahead. Never waste money on the biggest stock, as it will transplant poorly. In April buy plants which have rooted firmly into the soil in their polythene container. Try not to plant them where you will bother them by digging or rooting up weeds and bedding plants around them. They deserve to be isolated in a lawn or against a wall. Dig out a wide hole, about two yards wide, and fork leaf-mould and rotted manure down to a depth of three feet. You will be repaid by quicker growth and flower. Magnolias have a healthy appetite and like a lime-free general fertiliser every autumn. They move more easily in spring.

When choosing your example, you must assess your soil's degree of lime and your preference for tulip-flowers over strap-shaped ones. I have to reserve the smaller strap-shaped varieties for large tubs because their most manageable form prefers a slightly acid soil. It is so good in a tub that I will begin with it. *Magnolia stellata* will seldom grow more than six feet high and as many feet across. It flowers generously from an early age when a foot or so high. It is the white magnolia which you often see in suburban front gardens against the low boundary wall or beside the front path. Buy it, but be aware of its slow growth and small scale. The home of this shrub is confined to one mountain area in north-east Japan which it left for our gardens about a hundred years ago. The authority, Mr Bean, to whom I owe this point, goes on to remark that *stellata* should be underplanted with groups of a dark-blue grape hyacinth whose flowering season coincides with its own. *Stellata* sets its buds profusely along the bare branches and flowers elegantly before the leaves appear. Hilliers of Winchester list and often sell a special form called 'Water Lily' whose flowers are larger and more thickly 'tepalled'. It is worth the price, though others, pink and white also claim this name. Plain *stellata* is good enough, and even if its open flowers and thin white tepals are sometimes spoilt by heavy rain or frost, it is quick to replace them with a second crop. When the flowers age, they open out and begin to bend their narrow tepals backwards, fading like the similar petals on the lily-flowered tulips with which I prefer to match them. Its roots revel in a spongy, acid bed of leafy soil, but move more slowly, I find, in lime. As pot plants, they are seldom seen in Britain but the Japanese have long used them in tubs, as I now do. They once gave the plant the name Magnolia of the Houses because they brought it indoors so often. As its flowers are scented, it is worth putting up some young plants.

Among the bigger, strap-shaped varieties there is some recent news, which still seems to pass many new gardens by. Thirteen years, for a Magnolia, are but the twinkling of an eye, but in 1969 a form called 'Leonard Messel' took the RHS's [Royal Horticultural Society] highest award. It has a pale-pink flush to its petals and boasts *stellata* as one of its parents. Born from the most valuable cross among recent magnolias, 'Leonard Messel' is a variation on the desirable *loebneri*, the hybrid of a former director of Dresden Botanical Gardens. *Loebneri* tolerates all manner of soils, extending its tastes to lime and sometimes to chalk. It flowers, like its parent *stellata*, at a very early age, but it grows like its other parent, *kobus*, with unusual vigour and reaches ten or twelve feet quite rapidly. At thirty feet or so, it ought to stop. The branches are set with tepals like open stars before the leaves appear and in the 'Leonard Messel' form, their pink blossom is best viewed in half shade against the darker background of your wild shrubs. Among Camellias, it looks appropriate, but it will dignify a lime soil too and will put up with quite sharp frost when in bud. The pink form is even tougher than the white one. *Loebneri* and its variations have yet to catch gardeners' imaginations. They are easily placed in the further distance of any planting and lack all the slight awkwardnesses of many of their relations.

Lovely as the starry forms are, I prefer the large tulip-flowered forms of *soulangeana*.

These are the classic Magnolia trees, flowering on lime or acid soil, though turning a yellow-green in their leaf when the lime is very strong. There is a splendid flourish, often quoted, from their breeder, M. Soulange-Bodin, a retired cavalry officer from Napoleon's army who saw sense and turned gardener after 1815:

> It is to this that I cheerfully devote the remainder of my life. I shall not retrace the sad picture of the past. ... The Germans have encamped in my garden, I have encamped in the gardens of the Germans; and it was with sword in hand that I visited the botanical collections of Vienna, Minden, Stuttgart and Moscow. ... It had doubtless been better for both parties to have stayed at home. We are returned there, and the rising taste of gardening becomes one of the most agreeable guarantees of the repose of the world.

Of his parents' children, I dislike most of the forms with dark-purple flushes or exteriors to their flowers, as if their pure beauty had been dipped in chocolate sauce. That rules out 'Picture' and the intriguing new crosses on sale from Washington with bouncy teenage names like 'Ricki'. I ask only for a pure white, the exquisite form called *alba*, or for two fine forms with bold white flushes and varying degrees of purple, each of which is worth hunting down.

The finer of the two is called brozzonii. It is an Italian form which bears enormously long white petals [sic], nearly a foot wide when fully opened from their purple base to their white tips. This form flowers late, not until early May when the frosts are almost past. It grows just as readily as any other but is more spectacular.

The other, the older lennei, makes more concessions to deep purple. This large-flowered hybrid was born somewhere in Italy soon after 1848, though nobody knows where and one admirer is content to attribute it to the 'charming little bees of Lombardy'. Lennei's purple flowers have a white flush and a lovely white centre when they appear freely in late April. The tepals are fleshy to the touch and curve slightly inwards, giving you a strong sense of achievement when the huge flowers first appear in your garden.

Before me stands my vision of a better gardener, short of space, wary of large plants which may die in a hard winter, content with an alkaline soil and wanting a reward from this book within ten years. So I will pass over the marvellous evergreen *grandiflora* magnolia, fit only for British south walls and patient owners. I will urge connoisseurs with space and patience to pay for *highdownensis* (on lime or chalk) or the matchless *wilsonii* (best on acid soil). These are shrubs of an unbelievable beauty whose cup-shaped flowers are tilted downwards like the covers on a soup-tureen. Their leaves, when happy, are grey-green and as fine as a Tulip-Tree's. But rather than confuse or deter you, I will stand by *stellata*, 'Leonard Messel' and a white *soulangeana*.

Robin Lane Fox
Better Gardening
R&L
1982

A Salad Picture

JOY LARKCOM (born 1935) wrote this piece in 1984, when the rest of the country was more concerned with nouvelle cuisine and ruched curtains than exotic salad plants. It took us at least a decade to catch up with her. Now decorative vegetables, colourful lettuces and chicory are commonplace both in the garden and on the plate. I agree with everything Larkcom suggests, with the exception of the alternate planting of red and green lettuces – a bit too suburban for my taste.

It has always been one of my dreams to create a garden of outstanding beauty in which every tree, shrub and plant is not only lovely in itself, but is also edible or practical in some other way. The Americans have coined the term 'edible landscape' to describe the concept. I'm not sure I like the term, but I love the idea.

Salad vegetables must be the easiest group of plants to weave into an edible landscape, as so many of them are beautiful in colour, texture and habit. They can be used as eye-catching features, to create a tapestry of patches and patterns, worked into formal and informal flower beds, or used as decorative edges.

Probably the most handsome of all vegetables is the cardoon, with its lovely grey foliage and thistle-like leaves and heads, growing over 2 m/6 ft high. It is normally cultivated for its young stems, which are blanched and then cut in its first season. But it can be left in the ground and grown as a perennial. A single plant makes a magnificent focal point in a central position, or a row of cardoons can be grown as a hedge. The herbs angelica and lovage can be used in the same way; they grow into enormous, shiny-leaved handsome plants with dramatic seedheads.

Globe artichokes grow less tall than cardoons but have the same decorative qualities. They can also be planted in rows as hedges or used for demarcation purposes. So can the humble rhubarb. Though not, of course, a salad plant, it can make a handsome weed-smothering boundary to the salad garden.

'Feature' plants with misty fern-like foliage will make attractive soft-textured clumps. Examples are sweet cicely and the green and bronze forms of the perennial fennel, both of which will grow 1.2–1.5 m/4–5ft high. The fennels will combine beautifully with borage, though the latter may become cumbersome in mid-age and require supporting or trimming.

For colour in early summer, allow several chicory plants to run to seed. The clear-blue flowers open in the morning and close in early afternoon – a dramatic sight, as the spikes of some root and asparagus chicories can be over 3 m/10 ft tall. Red-leaved orach is used in salads when it is young, but any plants left to seed create a brilliant splash of coral colouring in the autumn.

Some of the climbing vegetables are very colourful. A good example is the runner-bean – first introduced into gardens as an ornamental plant. They and climbing French beans always look effective trained up trellises or grown up tepees of canes or strings. Exceptionally pretty is the old-fashioned variety, 'Painted Lady': the flowers are like apple blossoms. The purple-podded French climbing beans also have lovely dark foliage and mauve flowers in keeping with the pods. For additional drama climbing beans can be trained up trees or even up sunflowers – but firm staking will be necessary with the latter.

One of the prettiest ways of working a salad garden is to grow plants in small patches of triangles, squares or irregular shapes. The most suitable salad plants for this purpose are those with pretty or coloured foliage and a fairly even growth habit – coriander and red lettuce, for example – so that the patches look uniform rather than ragged.

Patches can be created by direct sowing of seedling crops, which are normally short-lived, or by transplanting young plants. For a continually full, tapestry effect, always have something ready to replace a seedling patch when it is finished. Some subjects, such as 'Karate', Mediterranean rocket, purslane, red and 'Sugar Loaf' chicory, can be treated as seedling crops to start with, then thinned to allow a smaller number of plants to mature.

Seedling crops with pretty foliage include garden cress, coriander, dill, mustard, alfalfa, fenugreek, curly endive and curly cutting lettuce. It's a nice idea to mix the seed of carrots and a variety of annual flowers and broadcast them together. The result is a colourful patch with flowers blooming among the carrot foliage. The carrots are pulled when they are ready.

For coloured patches, use red lettuce, beetroot and golden purslane and red Italian chicories – though these will only turn red or variegated in autumn. Very attractive dense effects can be created with salad rape, 'Sugar Loaf' chicory, green purslane and coriander – all of which can be direct-sown.

Vegetables which will make effective patches when planted are 'Karate', 'Mizuna', shungiku, asparagus peas, iceplant, 'Ragged Jack' kale, other dwarf and ornamental cabbages and kales and tomatoes.

It's great fun planning patches so that there are contrasts of colour, texture and form. And don't overlook the fact that intercropping can also result in very attractive effects, especially when there are contrasts. For example, small, round-headed lettuces are set off particularly well by the slender blue-green upright leaves of onions or leeks.

Edges in vegetable gardens should keep a neat, low profile. In summer, lively edges can be created with 'Salad Bowl' lettuce, especially the richly coloured red and green varieties, and the curly-leaved Italian 'Lollo' varieties, which have red and green forms. When red and green varieties are planted alternately, the effect is striking. Golden purslane and shungiku also make pretty edgings if picked frequently to keep them compact. In winter, corn salad, land cress and claytonia can all be grown as attractive edgings.

Many herbs can be used in this way. Parsley, which runs to seed after a year, and chives, which are best divided and renewed every two or three years, are traditional edging herbs. Let the chives flower in early summer – the purple heads look marvellous and can be used in salads – and then cut them back for a second crop. Sorrel and alpine strawberries make satisfactory edges, but need renewing every few years.

Evergreen edges can be achieved with a variety of salad herbs. Salad burnet, for example, though a perennial, sows itself annually. (The leaves of the young seedlings are more palatable than those of the older plants.) Other suitable herbs are hyssop (which is pretty in flower and has the merit of attracting bees and butterflies), winter savory, upright thymes, variegated marjoram and the neat winter marjoram, rue (renew it periodically with cuttings taken in spring) and southernwood (which will need hard clipping to keep it trim).

Edgings of flowers transform the appearance of a vegetable garden. Pansies will flower throughout the year; *Bellis perennis* (the double form of the garden daisy) in spring, summer and autumn; nasturtiums in summer and pot marigolds for much of the year. All of these can also be used in salads. *Limnanthes douglasii* (the poached-egg flower) also makes a cheerful edging, and attracts bees and hoverflies, while Chinese chives make a delightful permanent edging.

Joy Larkcom
The Salad Garden
FRANCES LINCOLN
1984

Choosing Colour

MICHAEL BALSTON (born 1944) *has won gold medals and Best in Show at Chelsea Flower Show and is as fine a theoretician on garden design as he is a practical gardener. In the following extract, he discusses the scientific reasons for choosing certain colours – and avoiding others.*

Our perception of the garden and its contents is conditioned by colour and texture. Different surfaces reflect either white light or selected wavelengths which we interpret as individual colours. If there is no reflection at all they appear black. Texture also is a function of reflection, in that a textured surface appears as a pattern of highlights (where light is reflected) and shadows (where light is absorbed). The coarser the texture the larger the areas of light and shade. Texture informs us about 'feel': a visual stimulus is confirmed by a tactile memory. While space and form determine our perception of the garden as a three-dimensional reality, colour and texture tell us all about its surfaces.

Useful analogies may be drawn between garden-making and interior decoration. Whenever we go into a room that seems particularly agreeable, in which everything belongs and fits well together, the chances are that it is decorated with a relatively limited palette of colours. These may be chosen to harmonize around one dominant colour, or they may contrast to give emphasis to one particular aspect of the room. It is unlikely that a room decorated indiscriminately with many colours, in which no one colour dominates, will be in any way memorable. So in gardens – though there is so much potential for colour, ruthless control is needed for the garden to become anything more than a mere collection of plants and ornament, however beautiful each individual item.

In the more fertile parts of the world, the predominant garden tends to be green, but that in itself comes in many shades, varying from yellow green to dark green-blue. Its intensity will change with the light from a misty, soft sage green to a vibrant, extravagant jungle green. The foliage greens already make a major impact in a garden, and any further colour must take account of them. Plants, of course, also have a vast array of flower colours, and often these colours are far from happy together. Rhododendrons en masse, for example, frequently stand and shriek at each other. Other elements of the garden, apart from the planting, also make their contributions. Large areas of structure may introduce whites, greys, browns, oranges, reds – even green or blue. Water may appear as a silvery-white non-colour, or reflect other colours around. Sculpture and furniture may come in a wild variety of unrelated hues. Now, if you are able to bring all these elements into harmony, the garden can be as thrilling as the beautifully decorated room.

Certain groups of colours mix well together, while others look unpleasant. Fashion to some extent influences our taste in colour, but there are also more fundamental relationships that have been objectively and exhaustively analysed. A basic theory of colour was formulated by Michel Chevreul in the 19th century, and has influenced discussions about the use of colour ever since. He was important to the Impressionists in painting, and to Gertrude Jekyll in gardening. In Jekyll's book *Colour in the Flower Garden*, she strongly emphasises the necessity for colour control, and gives many practical examples of successful colour combinations, using plants as the principal medium.

However, the application to the flower garden of complicated theories appropriate to the work of physicists, chemists or even painters is fraught with difficulty. Conditions in a laboratory or a studio may be relatively stable: light, pigment, viewing distance, surrounding colours, and so on, may be predetermined but in the garden there are so many variable factors quite outside the control of the gardener or the visitor. As you walk through the garden, viewpoints change constantly, so that colours are seen in all sorts of combinations with each other. The sun alters its position and intensity, throwing a deepening shadow, yellowing the garden at midday, reddening it towards dusk. The humidity of the atmosphere may soften colours that appear sharp and bright on a dry day. As the season advances, bright young leaves become dull and frequently turn a totally different colour before falling off. Flowers appear, then disappear, perhaps to be replaced by berries of quite a different colour. Despite these difficulties, scientific colour theories may offer a broad guide that can help in the choice of palette. For example, by combining hues that are closely related to each other in the spectrum (such as red, orange and yellow) you can achieve an harmonious scheme. Another way to create such harmony is to combine a hue with its tint (the colour lightened with white) or its shade (the colour darkened with black): red, pink and crimson would thus work well together. In dealing with other simple relationships, such as the complementary (opposed) colours red and green, you can again obtain satisfactory results provided that one or the other dominates.

More sophisticated colour schemes can be built around triads. This notion depends on the concept of the colour circle – an arrangement of the spectrum in a continuous wheel with complementaries opposite each other and harmonizing colours adjacent. A triad is found by rotating a triangle round the circle. The three primary colours – red, yellow and blue – make a triad, but produce the least satisfactory results when combined. However, by shifting round the colour circle to less fierce colours, you can obtain more subtle and interesting combinations: citrus, russet and slate, or buff, plum and sage, are commonly recommended. Remember, though, that green must form part of the group – unless it is a garden in which green is eliminated.

Michael Balston
The Well-Furnished Garden
MITCHELL BEAZLEY
1986

Weed Killer

ALAN BLOOM (1906–2005), *founder of the perennial nursery Blooms of Bressingham in Norfolk, was a man who was a truly practical gardener. His wisdom comes first-hand and can be trusted. Here he writes about how to tackle the weeds that gardeners dread the most.*

We gardeners seldom bother to observe the processes by which nature takes over a plot or piece of land which has been neglected or devastated. Some plant growth will appear even where there would appear to be no fertility whatever. It may take years before perennials, grass, weeds, shrubs or trees colonise it completely, but the law of survival of the fittest sees colonisation completed sooner or later. In a neglected garden this takes place much quicker than on an arid plot. In a matter of weeks a spick-and-span garden can be an unholy tangle with weeds competing with plants for light and nutriment, presenting a daunting task to the would-be rescuer.

Just as perennials eventually dominate a wholly neglected plot, so they will do the same in a neglected garden. It is these perennial weeds that are the greatest menace to gardeners, for however thickly annual weeds come up, they can be killed off provided the slaughter with a hoe begins while they are tiny. The best time of all for a quick, easy kill of these is when they are almost too small to see. This applies to perennial weeds, too, if they are seedlings, as usually they are mixed in with the annuals. Most garden soils contain enough viable weed seeds, just waiting for the chance to germinate, to produce a fresh crop of seedlings every time the soil is turned over or even disturbed. 'One year's seeding is seven year's weeding' is an adage worth remembering for it is true. Weeds such as groundsel can produce several generations in a single year if allowed to do so. Annual stinging nettles can produce and drop seeds all the year round and lose little of their vitality whether on the surface or dug in to germinate at a future date. I have known deep digging to produce different kinds of weeds to those which have been growing on that particular piece of ground before, and I believe Darwin found some fifty different weeds came up from the soil he scraped from a shot pheasant's feet.

From the standpoint of a specialist in perennials and alpines, the case against using chemical weed-killers is overwhelming. Their use on a bare piece of ground is all right so long as instructions are followed. But where a bed or border is already planted, then it is not merely dangerous but less effective than hoeing, even if the plants are carefully masked or avoided. A contact weed-killer can be used over dormant, leafless plants, but I find even then that it creates a film which inhibits aeration and needs to be stirred with a hoe within a few weeks. Some systemic weed-killers are designed to make a complete kill, and, even if they are reputed to be selective, it is seldom safe to use them where other plants are growing when the objective is to kill some deep-rooting perennial weed.

Which brings me to perennial weeds. One of these, the lesser celandine, I would not wish to eliminate, troublesome though it is in my garden. Its shiny, rounded deep-green leaves are a perfect complement to its cheerful yellow flowers in spring. If it were not a plant with such a nuisance value, I would want to grow it, or I would try to isolate it somewhere if I could for I would miss its welcome to spring. Usually I let it flower and then try to fork it out before seeding takes place. This is enough when it is growing between other plants, but well nigh impossible when it is established with its tiny, claw like white roots in with some clumpy subject.

That said, I would hesitate to say which is the worst perennial weed I am at war with. Ground elder (bishop's weed), marestail (or horsetail) and the larger bindweed or bell vine are for me the most persistent and difficult to control. All in their various ways are insidious, pernicious and destructive. Ground elder is seldom killed by merely one dose of systemic weed-killer and will lurk in the rootstock of other plants or hard-wood growth, ready to sally forth again. For this reason other remedies such as smothering with black polythene are also likely to be ineffective. The menace of marestail is its rapid spread from its black roots which delve so deep that no fork can ever reach them. I have known them to go under gravel paths and the foundations of walls to appear on the other side. It has no leaves to absorb a weed-killer effectively, but bruising or treading over the stems before treatment is helpful. To use a special impregnated glove may be the method to adopt for a small infestation, but spray after spray, maybe year after year, where it is dense or widespread, usually works.

Bindweed is in the same category as marestail. It has very deep and widely penetrating white roots and no amount of digging them out seems to reduce its vigour. This, too, will lurk in some permanent host. My worst patch has its home base in an ancient honeysuckle, and time and again has spread out from there. It is leafy enough to take weed-killer and will quickly show its effects. But while strangling (as its tentacles do) the stems of other plants, one is apt to avoid giving a complete overall dosage, which would make a surer kill if repeated often enough.

Another quite pretty weed is oxalis. The plural should be used here, for there are three of them. Not that any are common so far as I know but they could become so. The clover-leaved species has occasional salmon-pink flowers only three to four inches tall. The tiny bulbous root is the real menace for it forms many bulblets which become detached and so enlarge an infestation rapidly. As it has a long dormant period from autumn to late spring, one is apt to overlook its malignant presence among other plants because, as already mentioned, it is quite pretty. So, too, is a little yellow-flowered creeping species which delights in insinuating itself among alpine plants. It is so diminutive in all its parts that, again, it may be overlooked and even admired for its tiny bright yellow flowers until it is too late to tease it away from a choice dianthus or saxifraga. The third is a larger, less invasive species, often with purplish leaves and larger yellow flowers. Its name is *Oxalis corniculata*, and for all his antipathy towards bedding, William Robinson mentioned that it had some value for this purpose.

For many the most malignant weed is couch-grass which also bears the name tweetch, wicks and speargrass, according to locality. In my experience it is not the worst of weeds, but it is among the worst when it finds a refuge or base camp within a clumpy perennial or the roots of other subjects. When that happens, then it is almost as bad as ground elder, and total eradication is unlikely unless there is total clearance to begin with. In a bare patch of ground, couch can be killed by chemicals if these are applied when there is ample greenery, but one has to wait weeks in case of revival before digging it out for replanting. This, I have found, is less effective than forking over the area in the first place, especially if one works with the weather. Couch is not deep rooting and if cast out with a shake on top, sun and wind will kill it more quickly than any chemical. And if the process has to be repeated once or twice more, it is a more satisfying job than having to witness its slow decay from poison.

A farmer years ago rather boastfully told me how he cleaned up a couch-infested field. He had bought it cheaply because it was so foul. It was during the depression of the 1920s and the previous owner had done no more than plough and harrow to sow barley year after year, shirking a summer fallow which might have cleaned it out. 'I gave it', said the new owner, 'a proper smothering of mulch and ploughed it in with the couch. The next year all those little bits had grown strong and healthy instead of being starved like the land was. And then up it come with ploughing and pulling about until it was all on top, and, as soon as I could, I burnt it in dozens of little fires. Ash from burnt couch is good for the soil, and after that — well, I had crops like nobody ever had seen on that field before.' The point of this will not be missed. Perennial weeds such as couch are easier to master on soil of high fertility.

Alan Bloom
A Plantsman's Perspective
COLLINS
1987

A Gentle Plea for Chaos

I'm totally with MIRABEL OSLER *(born 1925) in asking for a little
disorder in the garden. I like to keep a few nettles for the caterpillars, ragwort for
the cinnabar moths and columbine seedlings where they choose to plant themselves.
But do not be misled by this writer's modesty. She gardens as beautifully as she writes.
Incidentally, the garden she mentions here, Rosemary Verey's Barnsley House in
Cirencester, Gloucestershire, became a hotel after Verey's death,
and until recently could be visited.*

Looking round gardens, how many of them lack that quality which adds an extra sensory dimension for the sake of orderliness? There is an antiseptic tidiness which characterizes a well-controlled gardener. And I'd go further and say that usually the gardener is male. Men seem more obsessed with order in the garden than women. They are pre-occupied with flower-bed edges cut with the precision of a pre-war hair cut. Using a lethal curved blade, they chop along the grass to make it conform to their schoolboy set squares, and with a dustpan and brush they collect 1 cm of wanton grass. Or, once they hold a hedge-trimmer, within seconds they have guillotined all those tender little growths on hawthorn or honeysuckle hedges that add to the blurring and enchantment of a garden in early June.

The very soul of a garden is shrivelled by zealous regimentation. Off with their heads go the ferns, ladies' mantles or crane's bill. A mania for neatness, a lust for conformity and away goes atmosphere and sensuality. What is left? Earth between plants; the dreaded tedium of clumps of colour with earth between. So the garden is reduced to merely a place of plants. Step – one, two. Stop – one, two; look down (no need ever to look up for there is no mystery ahead to draw you on), look down at each plant. Individually each is sublime undoubtedly. For a plantsman this is heaven. But where is lure? And where, alas, is seduction and gooseflesh on the arms?

There is a place for precision, naturally. Architectural lines such as those from hedges, walls, paths or topiary are the bones of a garden. But it is the artist who then allows for dishevelment and abandonment to evolve. People say gardening is the one occupation over which they have control. Fine. But why over-indulge? Control is vital for the original design and form; and a ruthless strength of mind is essential when you have planted some hideous thing you lack the courage to demolish. But there is a point when your steadying hand should be lifted and a bit of native vitality can be allowed to take over.

One of the small delights of gardening, undramatic but recurring, is when phlox or columbines seed themselves in unplanned places. When trickles of creeping jenny soften stony outlines or Welsh poppies cram a corner with their brilliant cadmium yellow alongside the deep blue spires of Jacob's ladder all arbitrarily seeding themselves like coloured smells about the place.

Cottage gardens used to have this quality. By their naturally evolved planting, brought about by the necessity of growing herbs and fruit trees, cabbages and gooseberries, amongst them there would be hollyhocks and honesty, campanulas and pinks. How rare now to see a real cottage garden. It is far more difficult to achieve than a contrived garden. It requires intuition, a genius for letting things have their heads.

In the Mediterranean areas this can still be seen. Discarded cans once used for feta cheese, olives or salt fish, are painted blue or white and stuffed to overflowing with geraniums placed with unaffected artlessness on steps or walls, under trees or on a window sill. Old tins are planted with basil, they stand on the threshold of a house, not for culinary use because basil is a sacred plant, but for the aromatic pleasure when a sprig is picked for the departing traveller. Under a vine shading the well, are aubergines, melons, courgettes and a scatter of gaudy zinnias. An uncatalogued rose is

grown for its scent near a seat where a fig tree provides shade and fruit. Common sense and unselfconsciousness have brought this about. A natural instinct inspired by practical necessity. We are too clever by half. We read too many books, we make too many notes. We lie too long in the bath planning gardens. Have we lost our impulsive faculties? Have we lost that intuitive feel for the flow and rightness of things; our awareness of the dynamics of a garden where things scatter where they please?

And this brings me to another observation which I think goes with my original longing for a little shambles here and there. For it seems that proper gardeners never sit in their gardens. Dedicated and single-minded the garden draws them into its embrace where their passions are never assuaged unless they are on their knees. But for us, the unserious, the improper people, who plant and drift, who prune and amble, we fritter away little dollops of time in sitting about our gardens. Benches for sunrise, seats for contemplation, resting-perches for the pure sublimity of smelling the evening air or merely ruminating about a distant shrub. We are the unorthodox gardeners who don't feel compulsion to pull out campion among the delphiniums; we can idle away vacantly small chunks of time without fretting about an outcrop of buttercups groping at the pulsatillas. Freedom to loll goes with random gardening, it goes with the modicum of chaos which I long to see here and there in more gardens.

Not all gardens fail, of course. There are two for instance which have this enchantment from the moment you enter. One belongs to people I know who live on the Welsh borders, where all the cottage-garden attributes such as mulberry, quince and damson trees grow amongst a profusion of valerian and chives, marjoram and sedums. The whole lush effect is immediate and soothing; it gives you a feeling of coming home, it reminds you of what life ought to be like.

In complete contrast is Rosemary Verey's garden at Barnsley House, near Cirencester in Gloucestershire. Here amongst the strong lines of design, parterres and walks, classical temple and knot garden, it is as if the owner had washed over the whole layout with soft, diffused colours so that hard lines are blurred. Sweet rocket and violas, rock roses and species tulips beguile, flow and confuse. It may not be chaos, it certainly isn't, but it is as if this truly cohesive effect happened while the owner had turned away her head. She hasn't, we know, for a garden like this has been painstakingly achieved from the brilliance of deliberation. Knowing when not to do things as vitally as knowing when to. There isn't a dandelion unaccounted for.

So when I make a plea for havoc, what would be lost? Merely the pristine appearance of a garden kept highly manicured which could be squandered for amiable disorder. Just in some places. Just to give a pull at our primeval senses. A mild desire for amorphous confusion which will gently infiltrate and, given time, one day will set the garden singing.

Mirabel Osler
'A Gentle Plea for Chaos'
HORTUS 3
Autumn 1987

England's Contribution

PENELOPE HOBHOUSE (born 1929) considers the influence of Gertrude Jekyll on twentieth-century gardens to be England's most important contribution to garden style since the landscape movement of the likes of Humphry Repton and Capability Brown. Here, Hobhouse explains how Jekyll's influence was achieved. Munstead Wood, the garden mentioned, is in Godalming in Surrey.

Most of us try to make all our garden areas perform for as much of the year as possible. Some subtle planting associations where bulbs and deciduous shrubs grow together can give an extended season. Small coloured anemones, scillas, chionodoxas and cyclamen thrive under the light shade of spring-or summer-flowering shrubs; tall stems of lilies will thrust upward through the spreading branches of low-growing shrubs; summer hyacinths, *Galtonia candicans*, can be planted between the rhizomes of sun-loving German iris. Daffodil bulbs can be grouped between crowns of hostas or Hemerocallis and emergent foliage quickly disguises the decaying daffodil leaves. Late-flowering perennial and annual climbers look their best clambering through the foliage of shrubs which flower in spring. The small-flowered species of Clematis or the C. *viticella* types, perennial or annual nasturtiums, and other annuals such as cobaeas, maurandias and morning glories will all drape woody bushes without causing damage. This sort of gardening is experimental and stimulating;

companion planting will make or break garden effects and skill in choosing plants to grow together lies not only in having a good sense of colour harmony but in knowing which plants will grow in similar conditions and give of their best at the same season. Most importantly, the time factor plays an essential role, more so in a mixed planting scheme than in any other border arrangement.

Generally speaking, annuals (plants which on the whole lack quality in their form and look best not as individual specimens but when massed together) grow quickest, reaching their peak in flower or foliage performance after a few weeks of being placed in their positions. Shallow-rooting biennials can often be reared in nursery quarters and only placed in their flowering site in the second season where they then, like annuals, rapidly develop. But biennials with deep tap roots resent this treatment: the useful ornamental thistles, onopordons, eryngiums, silybums and verbascums need to get well established during their first growing season. Honesty, forget-me-nots, foxgloves and evening primrose can all be moved to their spring-flowering positions in the previous autumn, preferably while warm weather and soil will help a plant re-establish its root system and encourage a further period of growth. Most perennials require a few growing seasons before they attain their full beauty, and most shrubs and trees need years rather than summers to develop their mature shape and form. Evergreens, which are the most useful architectural plants, are generally the slowest growers; they will not survive if closely surrounded with short-term planting designed for effects during the intervening seasons. Broom and Cistus, and bushy silvery-leaved artemisias and senecios, are quick growers but do not live long, generally needing replacing within the first five years.

This style of gardening, wherein informality of planting becomes a theme inside a quite formal framework, is typical of Gertrude Jekyll's many border designs. Much of her teaching relating to this aspect of planting, as conveyed in her books, remains as fresh and useful today as when she inspired the late Victorians and Edwardians to break away from their regimented bedding schemes. Few of the gardens she designed remain in a reasonable order, and at Munstead Wood, her own garden, only a faint flavour of her style can be traced. There, her nut-walk, stretching north beyond a paved courtyard behind her house, was typical of her simple planting technique. An avenue of the filbert, *Corylus maxima*, was underplanted with her own strain of Munstead primrose and other spring-flowerers, hellebores, anemones and bulbs forming a dense carpet at the base of the nut trees. At Hestercombe (which has been recently restored) her use of informal drifts of planting, inside Lutyens' elaborate stonework garden frame, is worth studying. On one of the terraces she planned a border based on plants with grey and silvery leaves. Lavenders and santolinas billow over edges and even cascade down walls in naturalistic fashion. Gertrude Jekyll was trained as an artist and was an experienced practical gardener; her taste and knowledge of plants and their needs ensured that, in her hands, informal planting inside the garden frame did not deteriorate into a purposeless jumble.

This sort of planting became the prototype for gardens such as Hidcote and Sissinghurst and has come to rival the 18th-century landscape as the most important English contribution to garden style. Other important gardens that follow this style are the smaller Tintinhull and Chilcombe, Athelhampton, Westwell Manor, and the more modern Abbots Ripton. Mountstewart in Northern Ireland and Crathes in Scotland are also superb examples of collaboration between architect and gardener.

Penelope Hobhouse
Garden Style
FRANCES LINCOLN
1988

Tulip Fever

When ANNA PAVORD (born 1940) wrote this piece, she had not embarked on her justly
famous 'biography' THE TULIP, a wonderful account of the eponymous plant.
But here you can see her burgeoning passion (which I share) for one
of the most thrilling and exotic flowers in the world.

I have been bombarded over the last couple of months with circulars from the bank urging me to borrow large sums of money to buy a new car or deck out the kitchen or build an extension to the house. None of these seemed worthwhile pursuits, so I wrote to the manager suggesting that he instead lend me a large sum of money to go on a tulip binge.

I am impatient to hurry on my life's work of growing every known variety of tulip before I die. He replied with a po-faced letter saying that, while a set of Formica tops or a kitchen cabinet were in order, he did not consider expenditure on bulbs the kind of activity in which the bank would wish to get involved. The man is clearly mad.

The problem is that so sure was I that the bank would enthusiastically endorse this endeavour, I had already sent off my order with cheque. We will have to cut down on rations elsewhere. Bean soup and biscuits must be the order of the day. If the bank manager had seen the border of 'Magier' tulips this spring, I am sure he would have been won over. Perhaps the thing to do would be to invite him over. If that doesn't work, I shall have to change banks.

'Magier' was the great hit of last season's tulips. It is a cottage tulip, or single late, as they are sometimes called, flowering through the second half of May. The petals are soft milky white splashed with purple round the edges. As the flower ages, which it does gracefully and well (a worthwhile attribute), the whole thing darkens and purple leaches out from the edges through the whole of the surface of the petals.

It is the most graceful, pleasing late tulip I have ever grown; tall – more than 2 ft/ 60 cm – but sturdy. None snapped. They more than made up for the sad disappointment of the early crocus planted round their feet in the same narrow border.

This was 'Ladykiller', a variety of C. vernus I had admired at the Royal Horticultural Society's show. The flowers were (when I saw them on the show bench) a dramatic combination of purple outside and white inside. In the garden, few came up, which may have been the mice's fault rather than the bulbs', but those that did had weak stems that keeled over as soon as the flower began to develop.

Much more fun were the fat Dutch crocus 'Remembrance' which burst from the ground with touching enthusiasm and taught me once again the important lesson that you can be too refined in gardening.

There was one disaster among the tulips too, a double early called 'Peach Blossom'. I had warmed to the double early after the spectacular success of 'Alice Leclercq', orange-red with a yellow edge. This is no longer available from Parkers, where I originally got it, nor from any other catalogues I have to hand, though all offer 'Peach Blossom'. This turned out not to be peachy at all, but a hideous and strident pink, with a formless flower. 'Squat and messy,' I have written in my tulip book. Unfortunately 'Alice Leclercq' did not prove to be a stayer, but I bet 'Peach Blossom' is and that next spring it will be there again in the front border, goading me for my foolishness in ever believing a catalogue description.

I am not giving up on the double earlies. Next season I am going to try 'Monte Carlo', lemon-yellow outside, deep golden-yellow inside, slightly taller than 'Peach Blossom' at 16 in./40 cm and flowering slightly later towards the end of April.

Although I have not tried it myself, I saw some good bowls of double-early tulips forced like hyacinths in a friend's house this spring. Used in this way, you could have 'Monte Carlo' in bloom by mid-February. To do this you need to plant earlier than you would outside.

Cover the bulbs with soil in a container and set them outside in a cool, shaded corner where you can cover the pot with a further 6 in./15 cm of earth. Leave them there until mid-January (with the earliest type) then bring them into a dark place indoors where the temperature does not get above 60°F/15°C. After two or three weeks, when the growth has been forced on, bring the bulbs into light and warmth for the flowers to develop. Either single or double earlies will respond well to this treatment, though some, such as 'Princess Irene', marigold-orange feathered with violet, need to be left outside until mid-February.

I have never grown the famous tulip 'Madame Lefeber' until this season and tried it in the same tub where I had previously grown the outstanding and similarly coloured 'Cantate'. Both are the same type of tulip, from the Fosteriana group, but I thought though 'Madame Lefeber' was good, 'Cantate' was better for it had much better foliage, silkily shining.

'Madame Lefeber' was a couple of weeks earlier in bloom, with long thin buds and greyish leaves. Next season I will try a different red tulip to go with the lime-green sulphurous bracts of the big euphorbia, E.characias. The Fosteriana type 'Princeps' is the one I have gone for, vermilion-scarlet 12 in./30 cm high.

It is perhaps contrary to assess tulips by foliage — leaves are not one of the family's great strengths — but this is an even better reason to commend those that produce more than a few tatty furls. 'Berlioz' had good leaves, like many of the Kaufmanniana types, and did well in pots by my back door. It has slightly pointed petals of good clear lemonish-yellow with a red base. The leaves are well mottled and streaked with purplish-brown on a grey-green base. It was very short, only 5 in./13 cm or so, but well-balanced, unlike the monstrous 'Peach Blossom'.

Anna Pavord
Gardening Companion
CHATTO & WINDUS
1992

The Answer is in the Soil

As GEOFF HAMILTON (1936—1996) *emphasizes in this extract, everything lies in the soil. Even the most badly conditioned soil can be brought back to life. I know; I inherited a London garden where the soil seemed to be dust, without a spark of fertility in it. It had been worked to death. A few years and a large amount of manure later, however, it was supporting a growing yew hedge, a greedy feeder if ever there was one. The only problem in London was finding the manure. We tried the Household Cavalry, but Buckingham Palace took most of what its horses produced. Eventually, we found it possible to buy 'heritage manure' created by the heavy horses at Greenwich. It cost as much as one of the horses themselves, so now we ferry steaming piles back from the country, where they can hardly give it away.*

The soil is a gardener's raw material. If it's treated with respect, nurtured, coddled and fed like the precious commodity it is, it'll repay you a thousand times over. In ancient times many civilisations worshipped the soil as 'Mother Earth', believing it to be the source of all that was good. They were not far wrong at that.

Mind you, if you've just moved into a new house where the builders have left you with a muddy sea of subsoil growing nothing but a crop of old bricks, bits of wire and hardened cement bags, you may not agree. But miraculously, with a bit of help from nature and a lot of work from you, even that can be brought back into fertility.

Unlike the modern farmer, the gardener should aim to create a living, breathing soil. In its natural state it contains billions of organisms, most of which are working away to your benefit to help produce strong, healthy plants. Of course, even the gardener expects far more from his or her soil than nature ever intended, so you'll need to put a lot more back in. But if you build that healthy foundation, a successful, beautiful and productive garden follows naturally and quite inevitably.

Soil Types

There are five major soil types that gardeners may have to contend with and each requires a slightly different management technique. In fact, most soils will be a mixture of two or more types and all garden soil should contain a certain amount of organic matter too, so it's impossible to be too precise. However, the nature of the predominant constituent will determine the type of soil you have to cultivate. Obviously, the first step is to get to know it.

CLAY

The particles of a clay soil are very small, so they compact together tightly, limiting draining and air flow. This makes clay soils feel smooth and sticky when wet, and hard as rock when dry. Nonetheless, they hold moisture well and, with it, necessary plant food. So, properly managed, clay soils will produce excellent plants in the end.

SAND

Relatively large particles put this type of soil at the other end of the range. Sandy soils feel rough and are gritty to the touch and are very well drained and aerated. They therefore need constant feeding and watering. But they warm up quickly and can be easily cultivated at most times of the year and always earlier in the season than clay.

SILT

This is soil that has been deposited by a river. The particles are small giving the soil a soft and silky feel when rubbed between the fingers. Like clay, silt has the disadvantages of bad draining and aeration but can be improved in the same way.

CHALK

One of the most restricting soils because the gritty nature and large particles make it free-draining and hungry like sand. Alas chalk soil is also very limey, so the range of plants it will support is somewhat limited. It has a pale appearance and often white lumps of free chalk can be seen. However, with diligent cultivation and careful choice of plants, chalk soil can still support excellent growth.

PEAT

Some of the world's best farming land was originally peat bog, so this soil can produce excellent growth. It's dark brown or black and feels wet and spongy to the touch. It can be difficult to manage in that it often lies wet in winter and dries out fast in summer. Its acid nature makes liming necessary for most plants.

LOAM

This is the common name for a mixture of soils and is what most gardeners will find in their plot. Heavy loams have a predominance of clay, while light loams are mainly sand. All contain organic matter. After a few years of good cultivation, all but the very extreme garden soils will eventually become what gardeners dream of – good loam.

Treatment of Different Soil Types

Even the heaviest blue clay, the rockiest mountainside or the squelchiest bog can be turned into a beautiful and satisfying garden – eventually. I make no pretence that it's easy or that it's quick. Heavy clay can take at least a couple of years to become workable, while the lightest sand or chalk soils need applications of organic matter every year – forever. But the rewards are great.

Bear in mind, too, that just growing things in any soil will improve it. Roots break up heavy clay and hold light soils together. As they die off and the plants' foliage is incorporated too, they provide a home for soil organisms, all of which contribute to the improvement. So, even if you do nothing at all but cover the soil with plants, it'll improve year by year.

Nothing damages clay or silt soils as much as trampling all over them when they're wet. Try to avoid this by working off boards whenever possible. The first step to improve these types of soil is to incorporate coarse grit into the top levels. The grit should be at least 3 mm in diameter. The amount to use depends on the soil but should be about a barrowload per 2–3 sq. m. This will make a permanent physical improvement. After that, incorporate as much organic matter as possible each year and try to keep the soil covered with plants for most of the year.

Sandy and chalky soils can generally be worked very shortly after rain. Improvement consists of continued applications of organic matter whenever possible. On the vegetable garden or where borders are being cultivated, it should be dug in during the autumn and winter. During the growing season, use all kinds of organic matter as a mulch between plants. This will quickly be worked into the soil by worms and weather.

Geoff Hamilton
'Gardeners' World' Practical Gardening Course
BBC BOOKS
1993

Designing a Water Garden

JAMES VAN SWEDEN (born 1935), in partnership with Wolfgang Oehme,
is one of America's foremost garden designers. In this extremely practical excerpt,
he gives factual advice on creating a water feature, proving, as he writes, that
garden designing involves a great deal more than pretty planting and complex plans.
His point about over-scaling, rather than under-scaling, is very important.

Budget often determines how elaborate or simple a design will be. There are many varieties of construction materials for elements such as coping, retaining walls, containers, and lighting, and the choice of materials will depend on your budget. Simple and less expensive materials often are the most beautiful and enduring.

I begin the design of a water feature by first taking into account the client's needs. But my real starting point is always personal experience. We all want our gardens to be stimulating and relaxing, and to provide seclusion. Most of us enjoy touching and listening to water. Its sound revives me and often makes me nostalgic. I find that the sight of a dramatic water's edge expands and connects the garden to a larger world, while intricate detail ensures that the closer I look, the more interesting the scene will be.

A water feature should be large enough to inhabit the garden space in proper proportion. Such proportion is a personal preference, which ultimately must be determined through experience and the study of other gardening traditions. My travels in Japan reversed my opinion concerning the size of lily ponds in a garden. It is not unusual for a lily pool in Japan to occupy one-third of the garden space. Now I am convinced it is important to err on the side of too large. My first trip to Japan taught me that the bigger the pool, the better the garden.

I have also found that garden elements such as terraces, pools, and planting-beds appear much larger on a drawing than when they are laid out on the site, and that planters and containers in the water take up more space than you might think. An adjacent terrace, for example, should be generous enough to balance the pool's size and shape and to accommodate furniture such as chaise longues, dining tables, and chairs. Remember that guests will gravitate toward water during parties. Again, my rule is always to err on the larger side.

they will scarcely bloom. I can't imagine a pool in July without water lilies in full bloom, so I place the pool as far away from trees as possible and never on the north side of woods. Also, falling leaves increase the maintenance, and tree roots can damage the shell or liner.

I place the water feature in such a way that my clients can benefit the most from the sound and cooling of the water close by. Water sounds soothing and screens out unwanted noise. The cooling effect of water and plants is most obvious if the water is next to a terrace or deck. Evaporating water lowers the air temperature, making hot summer nights more bearable.

One last, very important point: before I begin I survey the site to ensure that utilities such as water, storm sewer and electricity are available. I also determine how accessible the site is for both construction and maintenance. Water from the house is needed to fill and maintain the pool's or pond's water level. Electricity is required to run pumps, filters and lighting. Concrete and dump trucks must have access to the site during construction. Of course, we have dug pools by hand where machines could not go and used the resulting soil for mounds and planters.

James van Sweden
Gardening with Water
RANDOM HOUSE
1995

Seed Saving

Using your own seeds appeals to a particular kind of gardener
(I am not among them). These, it seems to me, are the obsessive collectors, the train-spotters
and anoraks of the garden world. That said, in this extract, BENJAMIN WATSON communicates
the fascination of harvesting seeds, and as gardeners, we owe these people a great deal.
Left to the commercial seedsmen, many varieties of fruit,
vegetables and flowers would now be extinct.

I f you've never saved seeds before, start with one easy crop in your first growing year. It's very hard to go wrong with self-pollinating annuals such as peas, beans, tomatoes, or peppers. Concentrate on saving seed from only one variety of each vegetable at a time, and plant other varieties of the same vegetable far enough away to lessen the chances of accidental cross-pollination.

Once you've saved seeds successfully from these plants, you can then move on to plants that require more advanced techniques such as hand pollination or caging.

Save seed from only the healthiest, best-looking individual plants. If you like you can also begin selecting plants based on specific qualities that you'd like to perpetuate: earliness, disease resistance, drought tolerance, and so on. Mark all plants you've set aside for seed saving with a brightly coloured piece of yarn, tape or ribbon. For individual fruits like squash, tomatoes or melons, wrap the marker around the plant stem near the fruits you plan to harvest for seed.

If you aren't selecting for a single characteristic (for instance, the earliest-ripening tomatoes), save seeds from several different fruits or plants, then mix them together once you've processed and dried them. This practice helps to preserve the genetic diversity of a particular open-pollinated variety, which in turn helps future crops respond to a wider range of climate and growing conditions. If you plan to offer seeds to other gardeners through a seed exchange, you will probably be required to save seed from as many healthy plants or fruits as possible to ensure broad diversity. Try to select plants based on a variety of good characteristics, not just for the size or quality of the vegetable's edible parts: vigorous growth, abundant flowers, heat or cold tolerance, and insect and disease resistance are all important qualities to carry on.

The right time to harvest seeds depends on the type of vegetable and the length of its growing season. For most vegetables, though, the seeds will not be fully mature until after the plant or its fruits have passed through the stage at which you would normally pick them for table use. Snap beans should be left on the plant until the seeds swell and the pods begin to dry. Eggplants, melons, squash, and other fruits intended for seed production should ideally be left on the vine or plant until they are very ripe and almost ready to fall off. There are exceptions to every rule, however, and a few varieties of heirloom tomatoes come to mind. Several of these old-timers will actually begin to sprout their seeds if the fruits are left too long on the plant. To be safe, pick tomatoes you are saving for seed at the same stage of ripeness as those you bring inside for eating.

Some vegetables, like corn, require a rather long growing season to dry seeds sufficiently; sweet corn varieties, for instance, should stand in the field for at least a month beyond the fresh eating stage. Mature, mostly dry ears of corn can withstand a few light frosts in the fall, but if heavy frosts threaten, or if the autumn season is particularly damp and rainy, it's best to pick the ears, strip back the husks, tie or braid them together and hang them up inside to finish drying. Harvest other long-season vegetables such as winter squash or onions around the time of the first fall frosts and cure them in the sun to prepare them for storage. Since onions are biennials, they will be planted out the following season; corn and squash seeds can be processed anytime throughout the winter.

Different vegetables require different seed-processing techniques. The seeds of melons and cucumbers, for instance, should be scraped out of the seed cavity into a bowl, covered with a little water, and left to ferment for four or five days. At the end of that time, pour off the floating pulp and immature seeds. Rinse the good seeds, then dry them on screens or paper towels. Tomato seeds and pulp undergo the same fermentation process, except that it is best done outside the house because of the strong and unpleasant smell. Don't let seed from heirloom tomatoes soak for more than four days, since some old-time varieties will begin to sprout quite easily, thus ruining the seeds for storage.

Drying garden seeds properly and storing them in good conditions (dry, cool, and dark) are the most important steps in ensuring their long life and good germination. Seeds dry best in a place that's warm and dry and that allows for good air circulation. Use simple, fine-mesh screen frames (store-bought or home-made) to dry many seeds outside in the warm, sunny days of later summer and fall. Another alternative, one that I use, is to place seeds in an envelope and put them in a canning jar or other airtight container with an equal weight of silica gel. Silica gel is a fine particulate material that draws excess moisture out of the seeds. Several mail-order seed companies sell silica gel, either in sealed packets or in bulk powder. If you buy bulk, look for the kind tinted with blue particles. When the gel absorbs a certain amount of moisture, the blue particles turn pink, and the gel should then be redried by spreading it out on a tray and placing it in a 200°F oven until it turns blue again.

Remove the seed packets from the silica jars after they have dried for a few days to a week; overdrying can harm seeds. Place the seeds in airtight containers (for small seeds, I use old plastic film containers) and store them in a cool, dry, dark location.

A freezer or refrigerator is ideal if you have the space, but any location where the temperature doesn't vary much will do.

Most vegetable seeds remain viable for at least three to five years in good storage conditions. Notable exceptions are alliums (onions, leeks, etc.) and parsnips. Still, if you store onion seed in ideal conditions in a freezer, don't toss out seed that's more than one year old. It's always a good idea to perform a germination test before planting time to determine how viable your seed is and therefore how thickly you'll need to sow it.

Testing germination is easy. As a sample, pick some fractional portion of 100 (10, 25 or 50), then place that number of seeds on a double thickness of dampened paper towel. Roll up the paper towel, put it inside a plastic bag, place a slip of paper with the variety name inside, seal the bag with a twist tie, then place the bag in a warm location – on top of the refrigerator is good. Check the bag after four or five days and see if the seeds have sprouted; slower-germination seeds may take seven to ten days or more to sprout.

Count the number of seeds that actually germinate. If 9 of 10 seeds sprout, your germination rate would be 90 per cent. If 21 of 25 sprout, the germination rate would be 84 per cent. Knowing the germination rate of your seed varieties not only helps you plan for your own garden needs, but it is an important step in record-keeping if you plan to offer seeds to other gardeners through a seed-exchange program.

One final note: never plant all your seed of a given variety. Every year seed catalogs stamp the words "Crop Failure" across varieties that for whatever reason (poor germination, hail, drought, grazing deer, etc.) didn't produce enough seed to offer for sale. Given the unpredictable weather extremes that seem to affect different parts of the US every summer, it's wise to keep a 'strategic reserve' of your favorite seeds on hand in case of disaster.

Benjamin Watson
Taylor's Guide to Heirloom Vegetables
HOUGHTON MIFFLIN HARCOURT
1996

Trickery

Perspective trickery, as JILL BILLINGTON *describes here, really does work. Gardeners should think theatrically while applying this; raked stages and backdrops add an illusion of distance applicable to the small garden. One word of warning: don't overdo the false perspective or make it too obvious. Subtle is the word, as the author says.*

Small should not mean twee or bijou because this defeats the object of enjoying and feeling at ease in your little garden. Similarly, prissiness and over-meticulousness have the effect of emphasizing smallness. But you can have fun playing with reflections and tricks of illusion which confuse the boundaries and widen the horizons of your space. The use of optical techniques, involving line, scale and colour, can be surprisingly effective in creating real deceptions.

USING PERSPECTIVE

Perspective illusions have fascinated artists since Roman times. Wall paintings in Pompeii show complicated architectural background scenes which retreat in implied space. By the time of the High Renaissance in Italy, 'rules' for drawing accurate solids and spaces had been devised and linear perspective became all the rage in European painting. What has this to do with your tiny plot? By using those same rules you can deceive the eye into believing that your garden is considerably larger than it is – but, like painting, this works from only a single viewpoint. Perspective illusions are based on the premise that objects appear to get smaller as we look into the distance. Hold your hand in front of your face and look through your fingers at people across the room: you will see that they appear to be nearly as small as your hand. Of course, this is not reality but simply your perception of it.

Similarly, if you are standing on timber decking laid at right angles to the house wall, with the lines running away from you, the slats appear to get narrower the further away they are: if your view continued to a far horizon, they would eventually be seen to meet. In the same way, the boundary walls to either side of your garden also appear to diminish and get closer together the further away they are. From your viewpoint, the top and base lines of the wall appear as diagonals, tapering ever closer to each other. The eye accepts this, so we still 'read' it correctly, knowing that the wall is actually a constant height. But what if you design this into your scheme physically? What if you foster the perspective illusion by planning a wall which really does get lower at the furthest end of your garden, or if you gradually reduce the height of a hedge by clipping the top so that it slopes down towards the far boundary? From the house, the garden will appear much deeper than it is. If you are building a pergola overhead, you can decrease the gaps between the upright posts and bring the sides closer together: by gradually narrowing the width of the area beneath the pergola, the illusion of deeper space is fostered. Central vanishing-point perspectives like these reinforce the impression of depth most effectively if they are not obvious: it is the subtle reduction that completes the illusion.

If your space is really too tiny for the above examples to be relevant, linear perspective can be made to work in a simpler way. Try a similar effect at ground level by deliberately tapering the width of a path from, say, 1 m to 75 cm. If you are paving the garden with rectangular stones, lay them running lengthways from the house and use a jointing pattern to reinforce the lines, with the long sides mortared but the short cross-joints 'butt jointed', that is, laid tightly together without any mortared seam. The effect will be to emphasize the long lines at the expense of the widthways joints, increasing the garden's apparent length again. Laying decking in parallel lines at right angles to the house is a simple way to achieve a similar lengthening effect.

False perspectives make effective illusions when they refer to the human scale. Build features on the far wall slightly smaller than you would expect: for example a 'loggia' made to be looked at but not used, with three arches about 1.5–1.6 m high and a shallow depth of only 1 m will look as if it were sufficiently in scale with people to be functional, whereas, in reality, it is too small. Painting the interior dark will make it look deeper still. The inclusion of figurative statuary, approximately three-quarters life size, is another way of altering proportion to indicate distance, because the eye will assume that the figure is life size. You could foster this illusion by siting a statue at the far end of a tapered pool, drawing the eye to a supposed distance.

Reinforce false perspectives by making elements of your garden larger in the foreground and smaller in the distance. Regular slatted fencing can be imitated at the rear of the garden with narrower slats. Similarly, large-leaved plants like *Fatsia japonica* could be placed beside the house with the smaller, but similar leaved × *Fatshedera lizei* sited on the further garden boundary.

Jill Billington
Really Small Gardens
QUADRILLE
1998

Working with Water

CHRISTOPHER BRADLEY-HOLE (born 1955) *has won numerous*
gold medals for his modern and minimal show gardens at Chelsea Flower Show.
But his designs are firmly rooted in the ancient and Classical gardens of the past.
Like gardeners working a millennium ago, he is excited
by the possibilities of water.

O f all the elements that make a garden, water connects most strongly with the emotions – creating music, movement, sparkle, rejuvenation, reflection, coolness, stillness, mystery and excitement, and symbolising even more. Water has the ability to draw the eye and so become the focus of attention in the garden. It acts as a centre of gravity, a feeling of energy flowing through space. No wonder it is so valued in many different cultures. A central canal was a familiar cooling feature used in many classical gardens, and it is particularly effective when it is introduced into a sloping or terraced site. But water has to be treated skilfully and with restraint to achieve its magical and powerful qualities.

The level of the water is crucial: the golden rule in designing a pool is to guarantee that it is full to the brim. The effect can look very simple, but it requires intricate detailing to achieve this result. To ensure that water is flush with the top of the adjacent paving of stone, brick, or other material, it is best to use a rigid lining such as steel, instead of a waterproof liner. This liner will achieve an abundant, understated, and uplifting image. Another improvement is to design the pool so that it is continually overflowing into a channel at one side, set a fraction below the level of the main pool and connected to a return pump. The water is kept brimming, and the constant flow also helps to clear any fallen leaves.

Water's other wonderful ability is to reflect the scene around it. Therefore a still pool that is carefully positioned can offer double value. This invariably works best when the pool is of a simple shape, well proportioned and with the minimum of detail which would complicate the view. Sunlit reflections are the most effective. This works with any pool size, with the items to be reflected being either a well-chosen pot filled to the rim or a giant square set into surrounding grass. Reflections are strongest when the inside of the pool is very dark – painted black, perhaps, or a very dark green.

Water can also separate two parts of the garden, providing a physical barrier such as a wall or hedge but without the visual separation. A moat can create a special island within the garden. The Belgian designer, Jacques Wirtz, has used this idea very successfully in a garden at Kontich, Belgium. The only way over the canal is a handsome bridge, its appearance narrowed by surrounding reeds, which heighten the experience of the separation.

But the most excitement comes from the movement of water. The sound and the sparkle are invaluable qualities, animating a restful space without affecting the mood of tranquillity. This is best seen in the classical water gardens at Villa d'Este [in Italy], where the terrace of one hundred fountains features carved stone gargoyles of every description. Fountain jets within the pool can create a wonderful effect, with individual jets designed to cross one another in a misty veil. In a contemporary design the jets can be set within paving, and computer operated to emerge in a series, with the water returning via drainage channels.

Christopher Bradley-Hole
The Minimalist Garden
MITCHELL BEAZLEY
1999

Gardens I Admire

DAVID HICKS (1929–1998) was a world-famous interior designer who became fascinated
by the design of gardens. He had very strong views (the book from which this extract is
taken contains a chapter of vituperation that I thought too daunting to include here).
He was quite an intimidating man, but he showed me round his Oxfordshire garden,
The Grove, which was beautiful and clever enough that
one could forgive him anything.

One of my great pleasures is to travel and discover new friends with a similar passion for their gardens in far-flung corners of the globe. And I am just as happy to drive over to someone in the next county and see how their roses are coming on.

I was brought up in a world of gardening and my ideas come from what I have seen in other people's gardens – in Australia, India, America and South Africa as well as Europe.

Planning and planting in a stylish way make up good garden design. It is no use having small groups of plants mixed up together; you must be very bold in your planting. If you have old-fashioned roses, have a lot of them, the massing of plants is very important. If you have a formal rose bed make sure that all the roses are the same colour, or at least are planted in blocks of colour.

Design is the essence of a good garden. Gardens should be like houses and have rooms; spaces should be contained by hedges, walls, fences or rows of trees.

A letter I wrote to a client in England in February 1990 sums up many of my thoughts and feelings about the sorts of gardens I admire.

> I am writing in the air between Johannesburg and Capetown. I thought I would take the opportunity to describe your garden as I see it in late June 1991. I have borne in mind that there will not be a full-time gardener so there will not be all that suburban mown grass and thousands of crevices between cracked bricks – perfectly hideous to weed!
>
> There will be no flower garden as such, no rose garden and no herbaceous borders but there will be twelve garden rooms, some of which will be furnished with accents of colour provided by old roses, new English roses and cutting roses such as 'Peace', 'Fragrant Cloud', 'Etoile de Holland' and 'New Dawn'. Other 'rooms' will be devoted to tree

peonies, fuchsias, buddleias and shrubs to provide autumn colour. In June you will be the possessor of a scented garden: honeysuckle, choisya, roses, jasmine, buddleia, viburnum, philadelphus, lavender.

The lines of chestnut, lime or hornbeam will be looking less like private-school people, and the grass on the recently levelled lawn will hopefully look like a Regency striped wallpaper. The terrace gravel will scrunch underfoot whilst the eye will feast on big squares of lavender and box and on climbing roses like 'Caroline Testout', 'Lady Waterlow' (so pushing), 'Lady Hillingdon' (always actively in bloom) and 'Constance Spry'. They are old beauties and I am afraid, like a lot of old ladies, somewhat demanding of one's attention.

David Hicks
My Kind of Garden
GARDEN ART PRESS
1999

First Impressions

Most gardening books assume that the reader has some knowledge of the subject and many assume that he or she is an equal expert with the writer. The book from which this passage by NOËL KINGSBURY (born 1957) is taken starts from scratch — as all gardeners have to do — and is full of the most basic practical advice. I have chosen this excerpt because it is clearly aimed at first-time garden buyers, who may find they have anything up to half an acre of land and not a clue what to do with it.

FINDING POTENTIAL

What is special about your garden, or potential garden? The first step in design is to analyse the garden's advantages and disadvantages. Remember that it will take a full cycle of seasons before the garden reveals itself completely. Look at your garden carefully and ask yourself some questions.

VIEWS

Are there pleasant views? If so, the best place from which to see them could become a good area for relaxing. Is there a distant view, such as far-off hills or a townscape? This can be made more of, for example, by framing it in a gap in a hedge or making it visible at the end of a path. Take a photograph of the garden and any view it has, and experiment with covering parts of the view with paper, to help you identify which are worth emphasizing.

CLIMATE AND ASPECT

Is your garden predominantly shady or sunny? Talk to previous residents or neighbours to get the full, year-round picture of the sunny and shady areas of your garden. Wherever the sun sets latest in midsummer is an obvious place for a seating or barbecue area. Sunny, open places are important for the more colourful summer plantings and herb gardens and vital for ponds and rockeries; shadier spots are ideal for spring plantings or cool, secret gardens. Dark, murky corners make useful service areas for compost bins and storage.

GRADIENTS

What about the distribution of flat and sloping land? A decent-sized flat area is useful for children's play and large-scale entertaining, but a smaller flat area on a slope has equal potential for smaller gatherings – views up or down add interest.

FEATURES

Are there any good aspects to the garden other than plants, such as a water feature, a patio or terrace, a pergola or a rockery? What about practical features, such as a greenhouse, cold frame or fruit cage? Although eventually you may change or move such items, initially you will probably wish to make the most of them.

PLANTS

Are there any good plants, such as established trees, younger trees that might grow to be a major feature, mature shrubs, borders and bulbs? When do existing plants flower or look their best? You may want to add other plants to enhance an already successful planting, or to 'fill in the gaps', for example creating an autumn planting around spring-flowering shrubs.

PATHS

Do the paths direct people around the garden in an interesting way? On a slope, routes are often dictated by the gradient, but on the flat you have more options about where paths should go.

DIVISIONS

How is space divided up in the garden? Large gardens may need to be divided to create smaller, more intimate areas. Are you happy with the existing divisions? What is the distinct character of each – open or enclosed, sunny or shaded?

INTEGRATED GARDENS

By now you will be getting a feel for your garden, but before you go any further you need to think about who will be using the space. A garden should serve the needs of all who use it, so the starting point is a list of functions – what and who is the garden for?

PLAYING: *children need some level areas for games, but love nooks and crannies and little windy paths. You may want to build a sandpit, tree-house or climbing frame.*

RELAXING: *this requires places that invite you to sit and unwind, which could mean enclosed arbours or spots with a lovely view.*

ENTERTAINING: *a site close to the kitchen can be useful, but you may prefer to put your seating or barbecue where it will catch the evening light in summer.*

VIEWING WILDLIFE: *this entails providing places where wild birds and animals can feel safe to feed and breed, and places from which they can be observed in comfort. A diversity of habitats can be offered by using a wide range of plant shapes and sizes.*

GARDENING! *You will need space for growing the plants you like, be they ornamental or edible.*

A successful garden is one that integrates as many of the desired functions as possible. Sitting on a patio is all the more enjoyable if the seating area is surrounded by beautiful, fragrant flowers. A pond not only makes an attractive focal point but is also an important wildlife resource.

Noël Kingsbury
Gardeners' Factfile
CONRAN OCTOPUS
1999

Designing with Grasses

The Dutch designer PIET OUDOLF *(born 1944) is king of the grasses, his designs depending on the waving plants used en masse. Here, he explains what grasses can do in a garden: how they remain true to nature. His point that they are especially unsuitable with roses is a good one. Grasses need to be left on the wild side.*

The use of grasses in gardens exemplifies the inspiration of nature. Long eschewed by gardeners, they are now at the forefront of planting design as increasing numbers of people begin to recognise their qualities, especially their reliability, long season of interest and tolerance of a wide range of different, and often difficult, environments.

Grasses possess special qualities that do not always fit into the conventional conception of the garden. They have a lightness of touch, a subtlety and an elegance that just does not look right next to hybrid roses, double flowers and bedding plants – the denizens of the traditional 'tidy' garden. Yet grasses are essential companions for the perennials that make up the contemporary garden.

Given their relative novelty, it is not surprising that many gardeners do not know quite what to do with them, and start timidly with the small, coloured foliage species, most of which are in fact sedges rather than true grasses: *Carex testacea* with its golden-bronze foliage, for example. Really to exploit the creative potential of grasses means being bolder and learning to appreciate qualities that previously might not have been considered important.

One such is the degree to which having grasses in the garden evokes a closeness to nature. Most open, wild environments are dominated by grasses; they form the foundation of many of the wild plant communities whose flowers are often the initial focus of our explorations of wild spaces. Simply having grasses in the garden immediately relates the garden to nature, forming a link with the surroundings if it is a country garden, or a timely reminder of wild places if it is in the city.

The effect of creating the feeling of nature is especially true of the medium-sized and larger grasses. Of the large number of varieties of miscanthus, *M. sinensis* is the most useful, with its neat, tall flower spikes that ripen to seedheads that remain a strong feature throughout the winter, with the asymmetrical look characteristic of reeds. Perhaps it is the most important border plant of the winter; combining delicacy with bulk, its seedheads are clearly defined even in the morning mist or the drizzle of a wet day. Species of molinia, calamagrostis and deschampsia are smaller than most of the miscanthus but are also reminiscent of wild places – grasses that could be encountered on walks along the woodland edge, perhaps, across moorland or through mountain meadows.

The ability of grasses to respond to light makes them invaluable, particularly in the winter, their subtle browns and yellows almost glowing in low winter sunlight while their seedheads can seem to catch the sunbeams. The soft texture and quiet colouring of many grasses, combined with the fact that they do not have colourful flowers, makes them a useful element in any planting, providing a rest for the eye, an opportunity to concentrate on some of the other, perhaps less dominant or demanding visual features.

Not only do grasses catch light from the air but they also respond very gracefully to the actual movement of the air itself. Indeed, some grasses are never still for more than a moment, either bending backwards in the breeze, or bowing down under stronger gusts of wind, they constantly bring another dimension to the border: the dynamic of movement.

The ability to capture light and movement are two special characteristics of many of the stipa grasses whose appearance is slightly less familiar to anyone who comes from cool, temperate climates. Their flower- and seedheads have a particularly soft appearance which perfectly complements the harder and more clearly defined shapes of most flowers.

All grasses have linear leaves which stand in striking contrast to the leaf shapes of most perennials, and they generally have a clearly defined habit, with radiating leaves or stems rising upwards from the base. This linearity and habit again make a most useful contrast to the habit of most perennials, making grasses a useful punctuation mark in the border.

Wonderful plants though grasses are, it is possible (as with everything in life) to have too much of a good thing. Placing different species of grass right next to each other is not generally visually pleasing; in particular, it seems that the different patterns of the radiating linearities of their leaves clash. Nor, on the whole, do they make successful companions for roses. There is too much of a contradiction between the intensely gardenesque nature of most roses and the wild beauty of grasses.

Piet Oudolf, with Noël Kingsbury
Designing with Plants
CONRAN OCTOPUS
1999

On Keeping Records

CHARLES ELLIOTT (born 1930) *is an American who gardens in Monmouth, on the borders of England and Wales, as well as being an editor and a writer with a fine, dry style. Garden records are important to gardeners – although I, like Elliott, always mean to take careful notes, but rarely do.*

A few years back I was helping my brother-in-law unpack some cardboard boxes full of books collected for a charity sale in New York State. They didn't amount to much, I have to say – a large contingent of *Reader's Digest* condensed novels that I wouldn't care to read even if they hadn't been shrunken, some high-school physics textbooks that pre-dated the A-bomb, a mysterious volume or two in what looked like Azerbaijani. But then I noticed a little black leather-bound volume full of clear, tiny handwriting in blue ink. It was, I soon discovered, a garden journal.

I often think of that book and wish I had kept it. I don't know who wrote it, but I suspect it was a woman because of the handwriting and the precision with which the entries were made. (Sorry if that sounds sexist, but that's what I thought at the time, and still do.) It recorded the usual things: the weather (particularly frosts), dates when significant garden events took place (the first early potatoes, new peas, lilac bloom), the names of flowers and vegetable plants. It also made note of chores that needed to be done and ideas for improving the garden, as well as comments on how some previous plans had turned out. The little book was clearly a labour of love, compiled with care and attention over at least forty years by someone whose garden represented an important part of her life.

One thing, however, made this garden diary different from a thousand others: it had been tossed out with the trash. This could only mean that the author had died. The chain had been broken. The fact that yellow tulips opened on 12 May in 1967 in Cropseyville was no longer of any interest to anybody at all, while the prospects for the new perennial bed behind the garage (new in 1958 that is) were, frankly, nil.

I still find this mildly poignant, but it does serve to point up the transience of gardens (to say nothing of human life). What it does not do is suggest that garden books and diaries are in any way a waste of time, just because the author may be the only reader. Keeping track of what goes where (or in far too many cases, went), noting successes and failures, setting down the details of purchases, sowings, harvests and what not, and generally compiling some sort of permanent record of this most impermanent creation may not be essential, but it's fun, and it may even have some practical value. I say this in the full awareness of my own failings as a record-keeper, of which I received a painful reminder the other day.

A year ago we made a new border out of a section of lawn overhung by lilacs and occupied by clumps of blind daffodils. It is big – 15 feet wide and more than 50 feet long – and as I was the one who wanted it, it fell to me to fill it up. This I did in my habitual disorganised way. I moved some plants from other beds – a couple of parahebes, half a dozen veronica plants, two or three buddleias, a couple of flowering currants, a batch of red and white penstemons Carol had started from cuttings, a large autumn-flowered 'Herbstfreude' sedum, which I split up into pieces, a smoke bush, one or two roses. Then I bought some more: a pretty little horizontal *Cornus controversa*, erigerons, *Coreopsis verticillata* 'Moonbeam', a *Thalictrum aquilegiifolium*, and four dahlias – two 'Bishop of Llandaff', a 'Small World', and a 'Moor Place'. Finally I started an unfeasible quantity of annuals from seed: flax, white cosmos, *Nicotiana sylvestris*, and what turned out to be entirely too much Limnanthes, sowed around the corners of the bed.

Last summer the border performed well, apart from some obvious overcrowding in places (the cosmos fell down on the dahlias, the nicotiana fell down on the penstemons, the flax simply fell down) and a few gaps where nothing took. In the autumn I cut away everything that looked dead and tossed compost wherever I could see bare earth. All was well and good during the winter, but then spring arrived.

The problem immediately presenting itself was that while the shrubs were easy enough to see, the perennials had mostly vanished. They were there somewhere, I was sure, submerged beneath a scattering of compost, chickweed and baby nettles; certain unidentifiable leafy clusters might actually be plants I wanted, rather than weeds. It was at this point that I remembered a clumsy sketch of the bed I had made last summer, hunted for it, and found it wedged in a jacket pocket. No map was ever more welcome to a lost traveller. The sketch allowed me to dig over the bed with reasonable confidence that I wasn't doing any actual harm. I even rediscovered – and preserved – a few late emergers (a clump of *Coreopsis verticillata*, for example) that I was sure had expired in the January freeze.

Now to anyone serious about garden journals and record-keeping, this must seem just a tad pathetic. Christopher Lloyd has said somewhere that you shouldn't even visit a new garden without a notebook in hand, and surely he is living proof of the wisdom of keeping track of what your own plants are doing, or not doing, under varying conditions. There may be people who can keep it all in their heads, but most of us are human. Besides, a garden journal can be, in its own modest way, a work of art, or at least something more than one of those places where facts accumulate like dead leaves in a clogged gutter ...

As a rule garden diaries are addressed mostly to the writer himself or herself. Thomas Jefferson's *Garden Book*, occupied as it largely is with notes on the weather, will never have the readership of the Declaration of Independence. Still, as Henry Mitchell in *The Essential Earthman* points out, 'a gardener profits from small trifling facts, and the more of them he has observed, the more resonant, the richer, his enjoyment becomes ... it is not the fact that is important, but the gardener's awareness that a fact is being beheld.'

Charles Elliott
The Potting Shed Papers
FRANCES LINCOLN
2002

Fashion

Fashion is as important to gardeners as to interior designers or cooks.
The craze for old roses took English gardeners by storm in the 1950s and 1960s,
to the extent that anything else in the rose line was considered horrid and vulgar.
With the benefit of hindsight, one can see that this fashion was as fleeting as all others.
JANE FEARNLEY-WHITTINGSTALL (born 1939) gently puts the craze in context.
Gardeners should always be aware that fashions and fads can cramp their style.

The Quest for old roses took Graham Thomas on a tour of botanic gardens, nurseries in Europe and America and private gardens. The latter included Chetwode Manor in Buckinghamshire where Mrs Louis Fleischmann had in her collection the rare 'Autumn Damask' and a fine, floriferous 'Tour de Malakoff'; High Trees, Chalfont St. Peter, where he found 'Cramoisi Picotee'; and the Honourable Robert James's garden at Richmond, Yorkshire, after whom the deliciously scented, rampant rambler 'Bobbie James' is called. Each garden yielded up one or two rarities. At Weston Hall near Towcester, Sacheverell Sitwell had in his collection the sumptuous crimson-purple 'Marechal Davoust'. Naturally, Major Lawrence Johnston's Hidcote and Mrs Muir's garden next door at Kiftsgate were on the route, and were much admired by Thomas.

Sissinghurst was an inevitable treat on the southern tour. Vita Sackville-West wrote the Foreword to Thomas's *The Old Shrub Roses*. She compared the colours of old roses to those of the carpets of Isfahan, Bokhara and Samarkand, 'rich as a fig broken open, soft as a ripened peach, freckled as an apricot, coral as a pomegranate, bloomy as a bunch of grapes.' The sensuality of her description is persuasive, but she also makes it clear that these are the aristocrats of roses. A taste for them is like a taste for oysters, acquired. ...

... The fashion for old roses had far-reaching effects. Gardeners who did not have a single Gallica, Damask or Bourbon rose in their garden were unconsciously influenced by the old rose cult in their choice of plants. Only a limited range of other colours flattered the dusky purples, magentas and mauves that Graham Thomas initially found so difficult to enjoy, and this limited colour range, with the roses they enhanced, became indicators of good taste. The only admissable orange-related shades were the pinky apricot and peach range exemplified in some of the hybrid musk roses such as

'Buff Beauty' or the China rose 'Mutabilis', neither of which are, strictly speaking, old roses, but they were acceptably refined in appearance. Harsher grades of orange and any yellow with the faintest hint of brassiness were greeted with an involuntary shudder although the pale yellows of verbascum and *Digitalis grandiflora* were recognised as the perfect complement to dark crimson and purple roses.

For nearly 50 years the gardens people envied and emulated were pink, blue, mauve and white with lots of grey and silver-leaved plants. Touches of purple, crimson and pale yellow provided daring highlights. It was a winning formula, and many of the most admired gardens today still adhere to it. Old roses, lightly pruned so as to produce billowing masses of colour in June, were an ideal component in formal beds with luxuriant informal planting in the Sissinghurst style. And, to emphasize the formal structure, the Tudor habit of edging beds with clipped box or lavender was revived. The style and colour scheme seems so completely suited to the English climate and light, and to the English temperament, that it has become a classical kind of gardening, from which gardeners may from time to time make adventurous sorties, but to which they will always return, as Englishwomen return, in the cycle of fashion, to flowery summer frocks and pastel cardigans.

It would be wrong to give the impression that a majority of gardeners embraced the fashionable style of the time, or took a fancy to old-fashioned roses. Roses were certainly the best-loved flower and could be found in one of their many forms in almost every garden. But most rose enthusiasts still grew hybrid tea and floribunda roses, in bush form, as standards and as climbers. Many gardeners were members of the Royal National Rose Society, formed in 1876. One of the services the Society provided was the trial of the numerous new roses introduced each year by hopeful breeders, amateurs as well as professionals. The popularity of many new varieties was short-lived, their faults becoming apparent after a few years.

Of the many roses introduced in the 1950s and 1960s, those that have stood the test of time include the coral-scarlet 'Fragrant Cloud', yellow 'Grandpa Dickson', and 'Pascali', one of the loveliest-ever white roses. The showy and perennially popular multicoloured red-and-yellow climber, 'Masquerade', was introduced in 1958, and the even gaudier 'Superstar', with its neon vermilion flowers, came in 1960. 'Who', the more fastidious gardeners asked, 'would want a rose with the vulgar colouring of a geranium?' The answer seemed to be, 'Almost everyone.' Among the best of the floribundas, bright, floriferous and healthy but mostly lacking in scent were the brilliant red 'Evelyn Fison', 'Pink Parfait', the tall, pink 'Queen Elizabeth' and two good yellow roses, 'Arthur Bell' and 'Chinatown'.

The legendary 'Peace', the most popular rose of all time on account of its symbolic significance as well as its huge pink-flushed yellow blooms, was bred by the French grower Francis Meilland at his nursery at Lyons in France, in 1939. Before the outbreak of World War II he was able to ensure a future for his promising, as yet unnamed, new rose, no. 3-35-40, by sending propagation material to colleagues in Germany and Italy. Also, by great good fortune, the American consul in Lyons was a rose-fancier, and when he had to leave in November 1939 he volunteered, in spite of a strict baggage allowance, to take a package from Meilland to the Pennsylvanian rose-grower, Robert Pyle. At the end of the war Meilland discovered that his rose had swept the board in trials in Italy and Germany and earned the highest rating ever in the All American Rose Selection trials. With a surge of post-war optimism it was decided to launch the wonder-rose under the name 'Peace' in 1945. Since then, well over 100 million plants of 'Peace' have been sold worldwide, assuring its place in garden history.

Jane Fearnley-Whittingstall
The Garden: An English Love Affair
WEIDENFELD & NICOLSON
2002

Keeping It Simple

STEPHEN LACEY (born 1957) *makes an excellent point: simple planting is not only easier but also more effective than complex. For my part, one of the most beautiful effects in my former garden in Halifax, Yorkshire, was created by the massed bluebells that covered the ground every spring, beneath a high canopy of beeches, their lime-green leaves just emerging. Needless to say, this was nature's gardening, rather than mine.*

It seems to me that there are easier and harder ways to plant a garden, and most of us instinctively choose the hardest. We grow too many plants. It is obvious really, but the more ingredients you add to a border, the trickier it is both to manage and to make sense of visually. So, when friends ask me how some piece of planting could be improved, I usually tell them to throw out ninety per cent of the plants. I enjoy the reaction. (I would like to have seen Vita Sackville-West's face when she asked Edwin Lutyens for suggestions, after taking him on a tour of her first garden at Long Barn near Sevenoaks [Kent]. 'Move,' he replied.)

Still, it is worth reminding yourself how potent and memorable the simplest planting schemes can be: a bank of daffodils, say, or a wall smothered in a white rambler rose. More sophisticated is the long, narrow stream of purple lavender, speared at intervals by dark, vertical Irish yews, that divides to sections of lawn at Mottisfont Abbey, Hampshire. Rich purple and grass green is an arresting colour mix. So is scarlet and green. At Penpergwm Lodge, Abergavenny [Wales], Catriona Boyle has planted a pergola entirely in green vines, with a fat clump of sword-leaved Crocosmia 'Lucifer' at the base of each post: a fine partnership even out of flower, although there is nothing there in winter.

Several Februarys ago, I went to a garden in the woods near Seattle [Washington] given over to hellebores. Four acres of hellebores. Its owner, Elfi Rahr, was completely besotted with them, so much so that after eventually agreeing to sell some of her offspring to a local nursery, she experienced such pangs that she went and bought them back. (The trouble is that every hellebore is different, with its own little personality.)

It was a drizzly day, but the garden was a wonderland, a torrent of nodding heads flowing down banks and around tree trunks to the edge of a lake, quiet enough still to be fished by bald eagles. Her simple, unmanicured approach was very much in the spirit of the place, unlike her neighbours over the fence who had suburbanized their plot with little lawns and flower-beds – not a leaf out of place. 'You can tell they are dental hygienists,' chuckled Elfi.

Another garden that haunts me is Lorna McMahon's in Galway, on the west coast of Ireland. It comprises a string of water gardens inside an old hazel copse. From glinty, peaty streams and pools, and sweeps of colourful astilbes and primulas, you walk into the dappled, mossy world of crooked hazel stems, sheeted with bluebells in spring, and with the remnants of stone walls snaking under the green canopy. One day I shall plant my own bluebell nuttery.

But at the very best, a garden needs passages of simplicity. One intricate border after another is a bit much to take. Somebody on my bookshelf (I can't remember who) compares it to serving up one rich plateful after another at dinner. Periodically, you yearn for a sorbet. An expanse of lawn, gravel or evergreen shrubs can provide it; in one Chelsea garden, the designer Christopher Bradley-Hole has planted an entire bed with clipped globes of box set against a sensuous wall of warm terracotta (achieved, in this instance, by brushing marble and mineral dust on to smooth plaster).

Among flowers, cool colours make the best refreshers, and a long run of a single species calms a scene nicely. Successive lines of catmint, blue irises and lavender terminate the mingled terrace planting at Gravetye Manor, Sussex. At Crathes Castle, Aberdeenshire [Scotland], mixed beds of crimson roses, purple-leaved shrubs, and orange and yellow perennials are interrupted by a stone bath, flanked by swags of old chain, foaming in nothing but lime-green *Alchemilla mollis*. And in a garden in Connecticut, James van Sweden has filled the view from the sitting-room with the most enormous bolt of white Japanese anemones (*A. × hybrida* 'Honorine Jobert') I have ever seen – well framed by the window's blue-grey paintwork. These anemones are in flower from July to October but further action can easily be programmed by interplanting with bulbs, such as snowdrops or daffodils.

Visually, perennials do gain immeasurably from being grown in a decent-sized drift, but I would only sacrifice the space to plants that either bloom for a very long time, or have appealing foliage. A hosta bed, for example, can be a stunning feature in shade, slugs permitting, with the blue and white variegated forms gradually blended into the green and yellows (again, bulbs could be massed around them in spring). The tall blue-leaved plume poppies, *Macleaya cordata* and *M. microcarpa* 'Coral Plume', create an equally impressive foliage sweep in sun.

In moist ground at Inverewe, near Ullapool [Scotland], the parasol leaves of *Darmera peltata* line the woodland paths like low hedges. While at Kerdale, in Brittany [France] rivulets of carmine and pink candelabra primulas lead into a green gulch entirely filled with the filigree shapes of shuttlecock ferns (*Matteucia*), backed by the giant rhubarb foliage of *Gunnera manicata*.

Stephen Lacey
Real Gardening
MICHAEL JOSEPH
2002

Hurrah for Horsetail

Gardeners who despair about this persistent weed in their borders might
be cheered by its extraordinary uses. MIRANDA SEYMOUR (born 1948),
novelist, biographer and writer on herbs, celebrates a plant
that is more than 400 million years old.

If you want to see horsetail in an intriguing setting, visit the old herb garret hidden away at the top of a spiral staircase above St Thomas's Church in Southwark, south-east London. This was where the herbs most commonly used in nearby St Thomas's Hospital were dried and dispersed. When the hospital was forced to move in 1862 as a consequence of the development of Waterloo Station and its incoming lines the garret fell into disuse; it was only rediscovered in 1957. The herbs you will see there today are those which would have been most popular a hundred and forty years ago: willowbark for stomach upsets, hops as a soporific, marshmallow and colt's foot for bronchial cough, comfrey and horsetail for healing wounds.

Horsetail's nicknames of shave grass, gunbright, scouring rush and bottlebrush plant indicate its most common function in the past: the scratchy silica crystals it contains make it a wonderful cleaning and polishing agent. The Romans used horsetail for their pots and pans, fletchers to polish the tips of their arrows, woodcarvers like sandpaper. Medieval housewives were so pleased with the shine it produced that they named it pewterwort. Dairymaids in the nineteenth century used horsetail to scrub out their wooden pails. Though long since replaced by manmade scourers, horsetail could still offer stiff competition – and it was apparently still being sold as a cleaner in Austrian markets in the 1950s.

The pleasing way the hollow stems can be pulled apart and put back together again in sections has earned it the modern popular name of Lego plant, but it's hard to verify whether horsetail was the inspiration behind the ubiquitous blocks. More certain is the intriguing fact that horsetail is descended from a giant of the Palaeozoic period (about four hundred million years ago). The Latin name, combining *equus*, horse, and *seta* or *saeta*, bristle, indicates that its resemblance to a horse's tail has always been considered striking, although nowadays we might be inclined to liken it to young asparagus, or a small, spiky Christmas tree.

If you fancy snake-charming, horsetail stems will provide you with a hand whistle which reptiles are said to find particularly alluring; horsetail stems can also be laid in a corner of the bedroom to increase fertility – or so the old books claim.

Horsetail has a solid medicinal reputation dating back to the Classical writers on herbs, Dioscorides and Galen. John Gerard quoted both as the sources for his commendation of horsetail as being 'of so great and singular a virtue in healing of wounds' that it would cure ruptures and internal 'burstings'. The stems of *Equisetum arvense*, the field or common horsetail, are the ones you need to make tisanes and poultices. Gather them in June or July when they are green and dry them carefully to ensure that they keep their colour, then store in sealed containers. To make a tisane, soak two teaspoons of the dried and chopped stems in a cup of water for ten–fifteen minutes. Drunk up to six times a day, it can help with bronchitis or any form of urinary ailment, and helps to enrich the blood. Mouth ulcers can be eased by holding the tea in the mouth for a minute, the mixture can also be dabbed on wounds, or on a cottonwool plug to stop a nosebleed. It will also soothe puffy eyelids.

Because it's good for the circulation, horsetail tea will improve the quality of your nails and hair. An old-fashioned cure for chilblains was to thrash them with holly until they bled; you might prefer to ease the irritation by drinking horsetail tea or dabbing it on the inflamed skin. Less usefully, perhaps, certain forms of horsetail store gold dust in their tissues – not enough to be worth gathering but sufficient to suggest there is more to be found – and the Iroquois of North America knew that its presence indicated a water supply. Gardeners, who despair of eradicating it from their borders, may be consoled to know that, mixed up in the proportions given for a tisane, horsetail makes a superb natural fungicide against rose mildew. It can even, it is alleged, be used to promote weight loss.

Miranda Seymour
A Brief History of Thyme and Other Herbs
JOHN MURRAY
2002

Growing Yew

The experiences of MONTY DON *(born 1955) with growing yew mirror my own.*
I have grown the plant as hedges in the Pennines, in London and in my present garden
in Suffolk. No, they don't like to be shaded; yes, they are much quicker than given credit for;
and, yes, they die when planted in puddles. I would just add that, once you have put drainage
in to remove the puddles, you will need to make sure the plants are not too dry.
Ours died first from drowning and second from thirst.
Our third attempts are doing fine.

No other hedge creates a better backdrop for a border or so perfectly defines an outdoor space than Yew (*Taxus baccata*). Evergreen, dense, retaining a clipped edge for 8 to 9 months of the year (it grows vigorously from late spring to late summer), it adds substance to any garden. If they are shaded – and no tree casts a deeper drier shade than a vigorous yew – then they grow scrawny and woody, although perfectly healthy. But if exposed to sunshine – even after hundreds of years in shade – they make a wonderfully dense tree. It is, of course, that density that we exploit by clipping it and making into a hedge.

One of the myths about yew hedges is that they are very slow to grow. This is completely untrue. Given the right conditions of rich, very free-draining soil, plenty of water and sunlight, they will put on a steady 30 cm (12 in.) a year and plants 45 cm (18 in.) tall will make a solid 2.5 m (8 ft) hedge in 10 years. However, it is true that it slows right down once it reaches maturity and they will reach an incredible age. It is now believed that the largest churchyard yew trees predate the earliest churches by as much as 2,000 years and that the oldest may be 4,500 years old. In other words churches were built on sites where there were already huge yew trees that had been the oldest and biggest thing around for longer than any cultural memory. No wonder they built churches near them.

The common yew grows best in the 'wild' on chalky soil but for garden purposes you can plant it in any type of soil as long as it has good drainage. This drainage is absolutely essential – as I discovered to my cost. I planted yew hedges in the front of our house with yew topiary cones. Everything was planted in a deep trench or hole half-filled with manure or compost and grew well for the first few years, putting on 15–30 cm (6–12 in.) of growth a year. On one side of this front garden the yew hedge flourished but on the other side I lost half a dozen quite large plants and another 20 or so became bronzed and ill.

My theory is that they have grown strongly through the topsoil but then they meet the stone foundations of much earlier buildings. Abnormally high levels of autumnal rain saturated the ground, so that the roots have sat in puddles on the subterranean stone and the plants were literally drowning.

I have not planted yew in our wetter back garden and if I had done I think that I would have put a drainage pipe along the bottom of the planting trench. With yew, drainage is everything.

I planted eight Irish yew (*Taxus baccata* 'Fastigiata') in the Jewel Garden to provide winter structure. It grows (very slowly in this garden) to make a slim column for the first 20 or so years of its life and only starts to gradually swell at the base thereafter. Like all yews it can be clipped hard back to the bare wood if need be so that it is the perfect evergreen tree for making a green pillar.

All Irish yews come from one or two female trees found in 1780 on a hillside in County Fermanagh. It is happiest in conditions similar to its original home, and grows taller and straighter in the wet West than the East, so there is hope for it in this wet, western plot.

Monty Don
The Complete Gardener
DORLING KINDERSLEY
2003

Window Boxes

Window boxes are a characteristic of London more, it seems to me, than of most other cities. ELSPETH THOMPSON (born 1961), *cycling around its streets, has an eye for the unusual and avant garde. Perhaps her sharp eye will encourage those who live in other inner cities to follow suit.*

Well-planted window boxes make a real difference to the look and feel of any house or flat, from both inside and out. From indoors, even grey buildings and greyer skies look better when glimpsed through a fringe of green – it's especially nice to have a window box that you can see in the morning when you wake up, or can gaze out on from the desk where you work. And from the street, window boxes not only make your home look beautiful and well cared for, they also provide a lot of pleasure for passers-by. Some may be so high up they can only be glimpsed from the top of a double decker or by craning your neck. But I love those tiny potted gardens in improbable places. Primrose Hill, Chelsea and the Barbican are good areas to go window-box spotting, but there is inspiration everywhere. Few daffodils have ever looked more beautiful than those I remember seeing along the window ledges of a concrete council block off the Old Kent Road.

Most London buildings have window ledges deep enough for a window box to sit on. Measure the space before you make or buy your planter – and go for the biggest dimensions possible, as this will increase the variety of things you can grow, and reduce the need for watering. Some of the troughs in the shops are terribly small, and will require a lot of attention if they are not to dry out. If your window ledge is narrow, it would be better to make or commission a taller box, which will provide more room for soil and roots – but not so high as to cut out too much light from the house. You may need a safety bracket to fix the box in place, particularly if the box is high up.

Terracotta, wood and plastic are the most common choices for planters, but galvanized metal is great for a more modern look, and there are some convincing imitation lead troughs from shops and mail-order catalogues – as seen adorning the smartest Georgian façades from Islington to Chelsea. Commissioning your own isn't as expensive as you might think. A good metalworker could make a galvanized trough for well under £100, and a carpenter knock up a nice wooden one for less. For our wide front bay window, a friend made me a lovely big box that measures 4 feet 6 inches long × 12 inches wide × 14 inches deep and is painted a sludgy grey-green that complements the different types of lavender that grow in it and the dark-purple paintwork on the rest of the house.

If you're going for a large box, check that your window ledge is strong enough to bear the combined weight of the box, plants and soil, especially when wet. You should make sure your planter has adequate drainage. Before planting, cover the holes with broken crocks and fill the bottom inch or two with gravel or lightweight aggregate so the plants won't sit in water. To improve matters further, sit your box on 'chocks' – small pieces of wood or little terracotta legs that are sold for the purpose.

There are two basic options when planting window boxes: permanent plantings that will remain in place year-in, year-out, and seasonal displays that will be changed two or three times a year. If you're clever, you can combine the two by leaving spaces in between the permanent plants for spring bulbs and summer bedding plants, but this can be tricky as the roots of the larger plants spread. A few years ago Guy Cooper and Gordon Taylor (more commonly known as the 'Curious Gardeners' from the television series of the same name) devised an ingenious window-box system that involved planting each plant in individual containers that could be kept in place or removed as required. Avant-garde gardeners that they are, Cooper and Taylor had the workings of their scheme on show, using clear plastic picnic drinks holders inserted into a shiny metal wine rack. But you could use the same principles with any old containers – even sawn-off plastic drinks bottles – that would remain hidden within the body of a normal box.

All over London, from barristers' chambers in Bloomsbury to smart Pimlico townhouses, you'll see versions of the traditional window box with a central conifer or cordyline, small shrub or box ball on either side and fringe of trailing ivy, with infills of cyclamen, solanums or bright-red salvias, according to the season. These are often planted and tended by maintenance companies, which may explain their sometimes stiff and regimented look. But a bold display of just one thing can look wonderful. I chose lavenders for my big front window box for both beauty and ease of maintenance. They are kept in shape by a good annual prune after flowering; I occasionally pop a few leftover nasturtium seeds in the corners for a bit of extra late-summer colour. I soon gave up on daffodils when I discovered that the dying foliage ruins the display. If you are clever, you can plant bulbs in layers, to come up in succession through a ground cover of ivy or mind-your-own-business — snowdrops and dwarf iris followed by daffodils and then tulips (whose floppy leaves should hide the dying daffodils) and even lilies. Low-growing ornamental grasses can be used to great effect in window boxes — they are easy to care for and the swishing sound and movement provide another element of interest. For a charity window-box auction I was involved with, the garden designer Penelope Hobhouse came up with the stunning idea of planting her galvanized trough with just one plant, the wild rye grass *Elymus hispidus*, whose subtle metallic sheen complemented the planter perfectly. Diversify your grass species and you could even have a miniature meadow outside your window buzzing with bees and butterflies.

The possibilities are endless — and the best place to look for inspiration is other gardeners' windows. One house near me has three terracotta troughs, one on each side of a big bay window, and in each there is just one plant of the mad corkscrew grass, *Juncus effusus* f. *spiralis*, sprouting from a mulch of purplish slate chippings. Another I pass on my bike on my ride into town is a froth of white pelargoniums cascading over shiny zinc planters — simplicity itself, but it couldn't be prettier. And sometimes more is more — anyone who ever saw it will never forget the eccentric window display in Percy Circus in King's Cross, where a window box spilling over with nasturtiums, French marigolds, salvias and other colourful bedding plants used to extend itself, via wall-mounted pots, wires and brackets, to stretch right around the window in a gaudy floral frame.

Elspeth Thompson
The London Gardener
FRANCES LINCOLN
2004

Creating a Vista

GEORGE CARTER (born 1948) is one of the most successful and talented garden designers working today. His signature gardens are classic and dramatic, with an innate sense of space (and an added touch of humour). In the book from which this extract is taken he gives detailed, practical advice on garden problems and pleasures, sharing with us his own skills and experience.

Creating a view or a primary scene in a garden can be likened to composing a picture. As in painting, it is useful to try and provide a foreground, middle ground, and distance however confined the space. This can be achieved by devising artificial divisions – the 'distance' may be only 6 m (20 ft) away, but if it is clearly defined it will work as the termination of your view in the way that a distant prospect works in a landscape by being framed by closer elements.

To create an axis, the eye must have an object or goal. Start by thinking where and what this should be. It might take the form of a sculpture or urn or even a small building; alternatively, it might be a distinctive plant or tree that stands well on its own. Whatever the focal point is, it must be clearly defined and have a strong, distinct outline. Remember that in nature, distant objects tend to be blue/grey – a result of particles in the atmosphere that affect the perception of colour. For this reason, it is better to avoid 'hot' red/orange colours in your viewstopper as they tend to jump forward visually.

The line of the axis needs to be decided in relation to the best features of the site – maybe the line should be directed towards the most open view, where the vista may act as a frame, or it could be aligned towards a view or object actually beyond your own garden. Alternatively, if you are placing a viewstopper within your own site, and if it is big enough, it could be placed so that it hides a defect – a neighbour's shed or intrusive window for example. The goal of the view or vista may not need to be a single object – it could be a change of scene such as a shaded plantation of trees or shrubs, or a planting of different character.

The primary vista ought to start from a point in the garden which will be constantly in sight — maybe a view from the sitting-room or kitchen window or from a prime seating position on a terrace or balcony.

The visual movement towards a view can be created in a number of ways. The simplest way is perhaps to mow a straight line of shorter grass between the two points, or to follow the line of a path. However, moving the eye in a certain direction doesn't necessarily rely on a straight line, and vistas are just as important in informal gardens: serpentine, or curved, lines can be just as effective, providing they terminate in a definite visual goal.

A vista does not necessarily rely on a visual movement at ground level such as a path or mowing line — it can be created by one or a series of frames. Think of flanking a view by a pair of dark trees, a pair of masonry or timber piers, a planted arch, or other similar device. The point is made more forcefully if there is more than one pair of framing devices — one set in the foreground, another in the middle ground for example.

You can have fun devising vistas that cross each other and are visible only from particular parts of the garden. They would also help to create that important element of surprise which is essential to successful gardens.

If you are planning a garden from scratch, it can be difficult in a featureless plot to know where to start and where to terminate a vista, but even in the most bland piece of earth you can be inspired by a study of the basic contours of the plot and developing your ideas from them. The principal windows that overlook the garden will give you the starting-off point for a vista. Then if nothing else exists think of the aspect of the plot. The direction it faces will have significant impact on the way light falls across the site and may give you a clue as to where to terminate a vista. A direct west-facing view would mean strong backlighting to an object in the evening, creating perhaps an interesting silhouette. Conversely, an east-facing view would be attractively front-lit in the evening. However slight the hint these site-specific considerations provide, they should be useful in formulating your ideas.

George Carter
Garden Spaces
MITCHELL BEAZLEY
2005

A Tool Kit

This advice from CLARISSA DICKSON WRIGHT (*born* 1947)
and JOHNNY SCOTT (*born* 1948) *about tools couldn't be
clearer or more accurate. Having cut my first lawn with nail scissors,
I now appreciate the advice always to buy the best once you can afford it.
To this list I would add my Jekyll weeding fork (apparently invented
by Gertrude Jekyll), only two tines wide and perfect for
dislodging such clinging weeds as dandelions.*

D on't stint on the quality of your tools or, as is always the case in life, it will prove more expensive in the end. Stainless-steel tools, though somewhat heavy, require the least maintenance and will last the longest, but they cost dear. If money is short, you can always start off with just a spade and fork.

Secondhand tools are another option. I often go to county shows and there is always a stall selling old tools. I have found some of my dearest friends on such stands. They are especially good places to find inexpensive trowels, hand forks, rakes and garden lines. They made things better in the past, so take a look. And remember, you can always replace handles if necessary. My marvellous weedcutter, similar to a narrow cleaver, is perfect for splitting lobsters. My gardening friends gaze at it enviously.

Dahlias

MICHAEL LOFTUS (born 1948) is one of the best nurserymen I know.
He loves his chosen plants and has dogmatic opinions about which to cultivate.
He is nearly always right. Anyone thinking of cultivating dahlias should follow this
advice from his extended nursery catalogue (worth having in itself), as I have.

Dahlias, named after Andreas Dahl, a pupil of Linnaeus, are the most gorgeous members of the Daisy family, but the original early 19th-century interest in them was mainly in the tubers as a potential foodstuff. Can you hear it – one portion of Dahlias and chips and make it snappy. Although originating in S. America and Mexico, Dahlias are of easy cultivation and much more hardy than generally supposed. If you are favoured with light soil, like ourselves, they will overwinter in the ground without any protection. For those doing penance for horticultural sins in a previous life, and enduring the rigours of clay, I recommend keeping your Dahlias in pots and plunging them in the herbaceous border. In November you can simply lift the pots and store overwinter under the greenhouse staging. They should be repotted in March with lavish additions of slow-release fertilizer; like so many tuberous plants, they are gross feeders. Dahlias, like Chrysanthemums, have attracted much baseless slander. Although there are plenty of vulgar and nasty cultivars, (from which the only gaiety to be extracted is in their demise. ('Hurrah ... it is a frost! The dahlias are all dead.' Surtees. Handley Cross. 1843)), Dahlias like 'Arabian Nights' stand up with the proudest of herbaceous plants. They provide an essential barbaric grandeur to the summer and autumn border (dainty Penstemons are not enough!), flowering profusely from July to November. Plant them with Helenium 'Moerheim Beauty', Crocosmias, *Miscanthus Strictus*. Christopher Lloyd recommends them for 'peppering up a haze of michaelmas daisies'. For admirers of *Cosmos atrosanguineus*, D. 'Arabian Nights' is a must. Its fully doubled flowers are of the richest, blackest red. Ht 120 cm. Sp. 40 cm. D. 'Berliner Kleene'. Decorative. Salmon-rose flowers. Ht 50 cm. D. 'Bishop of Llandaff' has pillar-box-red flowers and almost black foliage. Ht 85 cm. Sp. 40 cm. D. 'Dark Desire' is my current crush. Raised by Chris Ireland Smith, this is a plant of overwhelming beauty and grace. A chance seedling from the Bishop of Llandaff, it has rejected the grandiloquence of its parent and reverted to the wilding looks of its species ancestors. It has the deepest, darkest, velvety red, single, narrow-petalled flowers with the purest gold stamens. The foliage is finely cut and a darkish green. Ht 90 cm. Sp. 60 cm. D. 'David Howard' has deep-bronze foliage, which sets off resplendent, orangey-yellow flowers. Christopher Lloyd says this dahlia deserves 'every scrap of the praise lavished on it'. Ht 75 cm. Sp. 40 cm. D. 'Engelhardt's Matador'. Decorative. Large cool-purple flowers with black foliage. New to us. Bob Brown has planted it with *Artemisia* 'Powys Castle' and expresses himself deeply gruntled with the effect. Ht 100 cm. D. 'Grenadier'– another of Bob Brown's favourites. Very old variety with dark blackish leaves and double scarlet flowers. June–Oct. Ht 100 cm. Sp. 50 cm. D. 'Mermaid of Zennor' has, in the words of Bob Brown, lavender-lilac flowers in the shape of a hand with the fingers spread. The petals are long narrow and slightly twisted. Ht 75 cm. D. 'Melody Swing'. Decorative. Orange double flowers. Ht 50 cm. D. 'Moonfire' has dark-bronze foliage and single yellow flowers with a vermilion central ring. Ht 50 cm. Sp. 40 cm. D. 'Murdoch' is an old variety with stunning, exceptionally clear red, double flowers which open from gold bracts. July–Oct. Dark-green leaves. Ht 85 cm. Sp. 40 cm. D. 'Nuit d'Eté' has flowers of a similar colour to 'Arabian Nights' but the flowers are larger, of a small Waterlily type. Ht 100 cm. Sp. 40 cm. D. 'Beadnall Beauty' is a compact plant and has deep-crimson flowers and elegant black, more deeply divided foliage than the 'Bishop'. Ht 50 cm. Sp. 40 cm. D. 'Tally Ho' has single, vermilion flowers and black foliage. Ht 75 cm. Sp. 40 cm. D. *coccinea* is a fine species with variable orange, red or yellow single flowers. In Mexico in the wild it can grow to 270 cm; perhaps thankfully, in English gardens it rarely reaches more than 120 cm with a spread of about 50 cm.

Michael Loftus
Woottens of Wenhaston: The Plantsman's Handbook
WOOTTENS
2005

Garden Ornament

I agree with every word of this. There are some truly hideous ornaments out there. Not just gnomes – rightly banned from the Chelsea Flower Show – but grinning imps, pissing mannikins, gigantic concrete frogs and those unspeakable trees made of stainless steel. But, of course, gardens should have ornaments, for they are artificial and ornamental themselves. If in doubt, as TIM RICHARDSON *says, stick to the Classical. At least it's safe.*

Is garden ornament the love that dare not speak its gnome? It is a taboo subject in garden design because tastes vary so widely. That is the polite way of putting it. Garden designers know that when a client mentions casually on the 'phone that they have just installed a 'lovely figurine' purchased at the Hampton Court Palace Flower Show, they might as well have admitted to detonating a medium-sized bomb in the garden.

I don't want to harp on about how awful most garden ornament for sale is. That is taken as a given. There is of course a good deal of excellent stuff out there, too, and every designer will have their favourites. But perhaps it is worth making a few observations about ornament, if only as a tool for dissuading clients from going 'arty' and placing a frog wearing a golden crown in the middle of the lawn.

The problem with 'decoration' or 'ornament' is that the very words imply superfluousness. William Morris enjoined us to allow only the beautiful and useful into our homes, and functionalist Modernists of the 1960s and 1970s spurned all decoration. But why does everything have to be useful? Surely there is a place for decorative objects in the eclectic contemporary garden?

Such artefacts seem to work best when conceived as part of a coherent total design, not simply plonked down in the space to make it appear pretty or arty. 'Twas ever thus. Here is James Ralph, writing of statuary in *A Critical Review of the Publick Buildings . . . in London* (1734): 'A statue ... should, by its own nature, be suited to the place. To compleat an area, end a vesta, adorn a fountain, or decorate a banquetting-house or alcove, is the just and natural use of statues: not to people a garden, and make a nuisance of what ought to be a beauty.'

Good contemporary use of ornament and painted decoration can be seen in the work of designers such as George Carter and Anthony Noel. They show that strong decorative statements will work if they are consistently extended through the garden. Classical objects – either reclaimed (old) or reconstituted (new) – can work well if they are allowed to dictate the feel of the whole garden; we learned that from Harold Peto. Similarly, modern sculpture must be allowed to exert its power over a whole garden, as Jellicoe proved with the Sutton Place relief and the owners of Antony in Cornwall demonstrate with the complementary placement of a William Pye piece amid topiary.

The other alternative is to allow decorative objects to melt into the scene, to become part of the structure rather than stand-alone objects. Sissinghurst (which contains more decorative ornament than is sometimes remembered) is an object lesson in this, as is the Modernist use of large, gracefully aged terracotta urns as garden punctuation (see Ruys, Brookes and Aldington).

Perhaps it all seems rather obvious. But go to any garden show and you can still see designers falling into the trap of incorporating too many decorative 'voices' in a single design. It makes for a cacophony of the styles, and earplugs will not help.

Tim Richardson
'Garden Ornament'
Garden Design Journal
2005

On Watering

HELEN DILLON *is a fine gardener and, unlike some, her writing is direct
and unpretentious. In the book from which this passage is taken, she has chapters
for beginners, average gardeners and the know-it-alls. This chapter on
watering is for beginners, but we can still all learn from it.*

I often imagine meetings organized by manufacturers of garden tools. Earnest young men wearing black have stimulating discussions concerning the design of handles. But when the subject of the meeting concerns the design of the spout of a watering can, I suspect it's all about style and nothing to do with pouring ability (let alone colour, often a sickly pale green). The resulting cans cause water to gush out all at once with a hiccuppy gurgle, like a bad teapot. As a result seedlings lose their tenuous hold on life and even established pot plants lose the top half-inch of soil.

To me there is only one watering can worth having, and that's one made by Haws. It has perfect balance for lugging up and down the garden, and when you use the rose (metal thing with little holes in) the plants receive a gentle spray, like a benediction of summer rain.

Having water available on tap in various spots around the garden means that you don't put off watering something that needs it. In classic Edwardian gardens Edwin Lutyens had the sensible idea of providing dipping wells. We have placed large wooden barrels or dustbins under our taps as it's quicker to dunk a watering can than wait for it to fill from the tap.

The most soothing job in the garden is to stand, on a warm evening, holding a garden hose, aiming the water absent-mindedly at no plant in particular. It gives a satisfying feeling of hard work when it's nothing of the sort. I reckon it's the lazy sprinkle that probably harms the plants, by encouraging roots towards the surface, and it's better gardening to give each plant an occasional really good soak with a can. Plants in this garden that are watered very regularly by hand on summer evenings are clematis, delphiniums and dahlias. Each has a whole can – 6.8 litres/ 1 1/2 gallons. I once read that it was a good idea to sink an up-ended drainpipe beside plants that need watering often, so that when you aim the spout of the can at the pipe you can be sure water's getting straight to the roots. Taking this idea a step further, I sink pots (2.25 litres/ 1/2 gallon) into the ground near wall shrubs, with their rim at soil level. In spring lots of large tender plants, such as salvias, also in half-gallon pots, need hardening off in a sheltered place outside, and are inclined to fall over, as they are top-heavy. I anchor their pots within the sunken pots. I later remove the tender potted stuff and plant it out. All summer we water the plants in the notoriously dry wall beds via the sunken pots. Otherwise, water just runs, instead of sinking in.

An easy trap for beginners concerns the watering of containers. How many times have I heard people say that there's been rain, and therefore there's no need to water? Probably all the rain has done is make the leaves look satisfyingly damp, leaving the roots dry (incidentally an invitation to mildew). Even in winter (not in frosty weather) established evergreens in pots, such as camellias, bay trees and box, need watering. In summer, containers need an immense amount of water, certainly once a day and possibly twice when it's hot. A whole watering can per large pot is the ration. You often hear it said that watering should not be done when the sun is out, because the drops of water act like magnifying glasses and can burn the foliage. I saw this happen once, when a rodgersia was scorched. But I'd rather see the odd frizzled leaf than see plants short of water.

Watering under glass needs special care. Remember that apprentice gardeners in the eighteenth and nineteenth centuries had to have seven years' experience before being allowed to water in the greenhouse. Under glass in winter be very careful about watering when growth is at a standstill. By splashing water around you'll encourage grey mould (Botrytis), a fungus that thrives in close, damp conditions. In our greenhouse this disease turns up unfailingly every December, however fastidious I am about picking off dead leaves, tidying up and not leaving leaf litter around. Plants that are resting (pelargoniums and fuchsias for example) cannot absorb excess water and may need watering once a week or less, whereas young plants, such as autumn-rooted cuttings, should be kept just damp. Also it depends on the temperature of the greenhouse how much water you give. The colder you keep the greenhouse, the less you should water. (The water itself should be the same temperature as the greenhouse.) If a plant is overwatered it looks miserable, water doesn't seem to revive it and the pot is too heavy. Probably the last few times you noticed the plant was limp, so you gave it another slosh, thus ensuring death by overwatering (a remarkably common occurrence).

In summer under glass you should have an entirely different approach. Even when in a hurry before leaving for work, make sure to remember to open the ventilation. The temperature can soar quickly when the sun's out and trays of seedlings can shrivel fast if allowed to dry out. Damp down the floor, which means slosh water all over it several times a day. This makes more humidity and less of an invitation to red spider, a pest that thrives on dry air, and cools the greenhouse down temporarily. An interesting phenomenon is that on warm days in spring and autumn, by damping down the greenhouse in late afternoon, say four o'clock, and then shutting all doors and all ventilation, the climate inside becomes deliciously warm and beneficial to plant growth.

Helen Dillon
Helen Dillon's Garden Book
FRANCES LINCOLN
2007

Prince Charles's Kitchen Garden

THE DOWAGER MARCHIONESS OF SALISBURY (born 1922)
*is one of the best gardeners and designers in the world, having
been chatelaine of Cranborne Manor in Dorset and Hatfield House
in Hertfordshire, both of which possess historic gardens, and having also
designed gardens around grand houses the world over. Here, she describes
her work for Prince Charles at Highgrove in Gloucestershire.*

Some way from the house there was a large brick-walled kitchen garden, with a small orchard of fruit trees and an old circular pond which had been filled in, but little else. When I first saw it, it was a sea of mud, but it was a very promising space and it was here that the Prince wanted me to design a garden for flowers, vegetables and fruit, on the lines of the one I had designed and planted in the west country. My architect friend made a scale plan for me and I set to work to do the design.

The garden was to have four large squares with slender paths giving access to the beds within the squares. Each square had a different pattern of beds, and all was outlined with box hedging. Tunnels were constructed with curving metal arches rising from low apple hedges. The arches would have apples trained over them, and the narrow beds on either side of the central path were to be planted with hellebores and polyanthus, both happy in the half-shade. These apple tunnels, running from both sides of the garden, east to west, led into a large area outlined by a circle of standard *Malus* 'Golden Hornet', their linked branches creating in the spring a circle of blossom and in the autumn a golden crown of fruit. In the centre of the circle was the old pond, and here I felt there should be a fountain, but a simple one, no fancy figures or jets. I found what I believed to be just the thing in Italy, and, with the Prince's approval, it was ordered. It had a plain central bowl on a pedestal with a smaller bowl above and the water bubbled up to flow down into the basin, making a restful and satisfying sound. Here, I felt, unshaded and in full sun, was the perfect place for a garden of herbs. A double row of curved beds, edged in brick and with narrow paths dividing them, was laid around the fountain, and I planted the back beds entirely with rosemary and the front ones with a herb collection that the Women's Institute had given to the Prince and Princess as a wedding present.

The kitchen garden was a quiet haven away from the bustling life that went on in less protected places in the garden. The two young princes were tiny boys then – in fact when I started to design the garden, there was only one. Prince Charles had a low white-painted picket fence made to surround the fountain so that it was safe for them.

The paths in the four squares led into circular domed arbours and I have just found the list of the plants I put there to cover them, chosen so that two arbours would be in flower at the same time and all four would have something in flower. There were roses 'Seagull', 'Climbing Pompom de Paris', 'Albertine', 'Emily Gray' and 'Adelaide d'Orleans', 'Sanders' White', *Clematis montana* and three wisterias, *W. sinensis*, *W.* 'Pink Ice', *W. floribunda* 'Snow Showers'. The Prince had chairs put in each of the arbours, though it was seldom he sat on them, more likely he would, secateurs in hand, be pruning something.

The garden had a broad central walk running from north to south. Here wide borders were made and planted with roses and many of the Prince's favourite herbaceous plants. I remember ordering for him some dark-purple delphiniums which he especially liked, but there were herbaceous peonies, too, sage and grey-foliaged plants. Dennis Brown was the star of the show, for it was he who grew the vegetables, and magnificent they were. There is nothing, to my mind, more beautiful than an orderly kitchen garden and Dennis was the man to create it. With the vegetables he grew in his own garden, he had won every local prize that was going, and now the Prince was lucky enough to have Dennis growing his. I first remember Dennis in his green hunt coat whipping in the hounds on hunting days with the Beaufort, and keeping them in just as good order as he does his vegetables.

The Dowager Marchioness of Salisbury
A Gardener's Life
FRANCES LINCOLN
2007

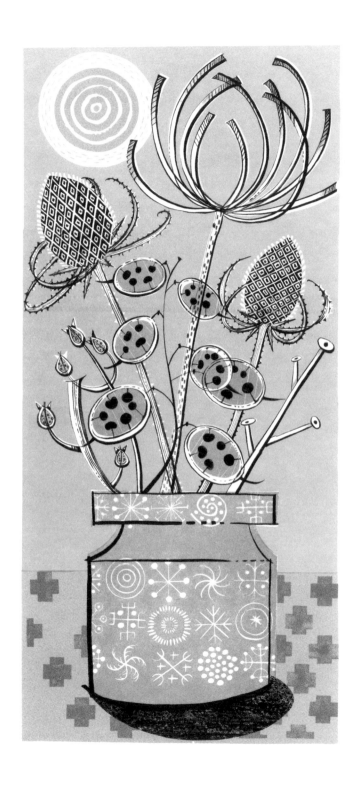

LESLIE GEDDES-BROWN is a leading writer on gardening.
Her books include *The Walled Garden* (2007) and
The Water Garden (2008), both published
by Merrell.

ANGIE LEWIN, a member of the Royal Society
of Painter Print-Makers and the Society of Wood Engravers,
has exhibited her work around the
United Kingdom.

First published 2009 by

Merrell Publishers Limited
81 Southwark Street
London SE1 0HX

merrellpublishers.com

Introduction and introductory passages copyright © 2009
    Leslie Geddes-Brown
Textual extracts copyright © the copyright holders;
    see p. 158
Illustrations copyright © 2009 Angie Lewin
Design and layout copyright © 2009
    Merrell Publishers Limited

British Library Cataloguing-in-Publication Data:
Garden wisdom.
    1. Gardening. 2. Gardening – Literary collections.
    I. Geddes-Brown, Leslie. II. Lewin, Angie.
    635-dc22

ISBN 978-1-8589-4462-3

Produced by Merrell Publishers Limited
Art-directed by Nicola Bailey
Designed by Jonny Burch
Project-managed by Lucy Smith
Indexed by Diana LeCore

Printed and bound in China

ILLUSTRATIONS

FRONT COVER: *The Moonlit Cup*, 2008, linocut

PAGE 2: *Weybourne to Sheringham*, 2003, linocut

PAGE 4: *Ballindalloch*, 2004, linocut

PAGE 11: *Goat's-beard II*, 2003, linocut

PAGE 19: *Clocks*, 2003, wood engraving

PAGE 27: *Scarista*, 2007, linocut

PAGE 39: *Two Green Jars*, 2004, linocut

PAGE 49: *Seedheads*, 2003, linocut

PAGE 55: *Agapanthus*, 2008, lithograph

PAGE 61: *Winter Spey II*, 2008, wood engraving

PAGE 69: *Autumn Spey*, 2008, lithograph

PAGE 79: *Wild Garden*, 2007, lithograph

PAGE 93: *Spey Path I*, 2004, linocut

PAGE 99: *Honesty*, 2003, linocut

PAGE 107: *Red Meadow*, 2004, wood engraving

PAGE 111: *Hidden Fish*, 2008, wood engraving

PAGE 121: *Island with Teasels*, 2006, linocut

PAGE 131: *Dandelion II*, 2003, wood engraving

PAGE 147: *Alliums*, 2007, linocut

PAGE 157: *Totem*, 2007, lithograph